The
Vegetable Growers'
Calendar

THE VEGETABLE GROWERS' CALENDAR

David Mabey

Illustrations by David Goddard

Macdonald and Jane's · London

Published 1976 by Macdonald and Jane's Publishers Ltd.
Paulton House,
8 Shepherdess Walk, London N1 7LW

ISBN 0 354 04011 1

Printed and bound in Great Britain by
Redwood Burn Limited
Trowbridge & Esher

For John and Rosemary

Author's Note
The quotations at the beginning of each month
are taken from *Five Hundred Pointes of Good
Husbandrie* by Thomas Tusser 1580 edition
collated with 1573 and 1577, edited by W. Payne
and S.J. Herrtage, and published for the English
Dialect Society by Trubner and Co. in 1878

Contents

Preface

Some time ago I was travelling out of London by train when I noticed strange sights on the embankment; regular squares of ground had been hewn out of the bank, and leeks and cabbages were growing just a few yards from the track. These tiny plots—some no more than a few square yards of ground cleared of grass and wild plants—were an encouraging sign, a small indication that some important changes were beginning to take place with regard to our attitudes to home produce.

These developments are, of course, partly a reaction to rocketing prices, but there are other reasons: the taste of fresh vegetables is more highly valued than it was a few years ago, we have begun to appreciate that the biggest, most perfect-looking specimens do not necessarily have the best flavour, and we are no longer prepared to tolerate the widespread contamination of food with sprays and insecticides. We are becoming more critical of what we eat, and rightly so.

Those railway embankments were a hint of change, but now the signs are everywhere: town allotments that were returning to the wild without tenants are organized and cultivated, neat flower gardens are being dug up and replaced by vegetable plots, and there is much talk of digging for victory, or even survival. This is quite understandable. The circumstances and the reasons may be very different, but the same spirit of economy and resourcefulness is directing today's 'new gardeners', as it did those of over thirty years ago.

Wartime gardeners, many of whom were new to the idea of growing food themselves, had a number of books to help them. One of the best known was a little book by the radio gardener, C. H. Middleton—known throughout the country as Mr Middleton. His guide to food gardening was sponsored by the government 'Dig for Victory' campaign. It is a splendid, but highly disorganized, book, full of curious advertisements and propaganda, and in the writing there are always echoes and reminders of a country at war, for example when he warns gardeners about the dangers of bonfires which are not extinguished before the blackout.

It was this book which initially inspired my own account of growing food. I have tried to retain the spirit of the book—the good sense, the economy, the imagination, and the urgency Middleton stresses. But, because circumstances are different today, my book also had to be different. I have developed his idea of a calendar, although I felt that his division of the year into weeks was too rigid; in my experience, a month is a much more practical and sensible division.

I have concentrated on a particular style of gardening. It is essentially outdoor, although there are references to greenhouses and so forth. The main scheme is geared towards managing a plot, whether it be a large allotment or a few square yards of railway embankment. I have also tried to give an overall picture of the problems and pleasures of growing food throughout the year; how each month has its own special character, dictated by the weather, the work and the crops, and the way in which the cycle of the year develops.

Another important factor, that I have stressed again and again, is the link between the garden and the kitchen. Since this is the whole point of food gardening, you cannot make full use of your plot unless you are aware of the importance of the kitchen; the two depend on one another. You must plan your garden to suit the needs of your kitchen.

How to Use this Book

The first thing to say is that it is not practical to outline every single job that needs to be done each month; the book would be boringly repetitive and unwieldy. Of course, repetitive work is part of the business of gardening, and should not be underestimated. So you must use your common sense when you read the book, just as you do when you are in the garden; adapt the information to suit your plot, the climate and the needs of your kitchen.

The main part of the book is a calendar beginning with January. This is an arbitrary but convenient starting point, although the gardening year has no real beginning or end. You can follow each month as the year progresses, but be sure to look ahead—not only in the book, but also in your planning —so that you are well prepared for important jobs to come. At the beginning of each month there is a brief summary listing the main topics and tasks, divided up into sections such as sowing, planting and picking.

Before the calendar there is a general introduction dealing in some detail with such things as seeds, crop rotation, and digging. You should pay particular attention to the cropping plan on p. 15, and if you want information about a particular crop, there is a chart on pp. 17-18 which shows when each crop is sown and planted out, when it is likely to be ready, and how long it will last. Check this, and then turn to the relevant month for more details.

A word about varieties. I have kept these out of the calendar, as too many strange names would be confusing. But on p. 19 in the Introduction there is a list of suggestions. Look at this before you start work.

Finally, don't treat the calendar as a rigid, inflexible guide. If one of your crops is ready a month earlier than I indicate, then you must adapt your work accordingly. The calendar is intended to be a general picture of how to handle a food garden throughout the year.

Introduction

Tools

Three tools in particular are vital for the food gardener: the spade, the fork and the hoe. There are many others as well, and the final contents of your shed will really depend on the ground and conditions that you have to cope with. Here is a basic list.

Spade: this is your essential digging tool. Don't confuse it with a shovel, which is meant for scooping and can't be used for digging. A good spade should have several attributes: it should be comfortable for you to handle; it should have a long flat blade with a sharp cutting edge; and it should have a solid tread above the blade. If you keep it clean and in good condition, it should be able to deal with the roughest work.

Fork: a fork is not normally much good for digging unless the land is full of wet clay, then it is useful. A large fork with four tines or prongs is best used for breaking up clods after digging, for forking over ground that has been dug, for moving manure, etc., and for lifting root crops. Like a spade, it needs to be comfortable, and normally a long-tined fork is best, although some gardeners prefer to use a fork with shorter, broad tines for jobs like lifting potatoes.

Handfork: a small version of the digging fork, very useful for weeding, particularly in places that cannot be reached with a hoe. It is also useful for lifting young plants where the soil is too heavy for a trowel.

Dutch hoe: this is a hoe with a forward-facing flat blade. It is ideal for general weeding. Use it by jabbing it forward and working gradually backwards. Hoeing helps to keep down weeds, it breaks down the soil and keeps the surface loose and fine, so that moisture is retained.

Draw hoe: another hoe, this time with a sharp blade fixed at right angles to the handle, used for general weeding like a Dutch hoe, except that the action is different. It is worked with a chopping action and you move forwards over the soil. A draw hoe is also useful for earthing up potatoes, and for making drills for planting and sowing.

There are other hoes like the Canterbury hoe which has a kind of three-pronged fork attached at right angles to the handle; also there are hoes with triangular blades that are useful for making drills.

Rake: another very important tool used mainly for clearing ground of stones, and for general levelling and fining of the soil. Turned over, so that the prongs are upwards, the rake can be used for filling in drills.

Dibber: a hole-making tool; usually made from the top end of an old spade—that is the wooden handle and part of the stem, sharpened to a point. It is used for planting out leeks, brassicas, etc., and also for sowing crops like broad beans when drills are not used. Its only disadvantage is that it produces a tapering hole, and if you are not careful, seeds or plants may hang without anchorage for some time after planting. So it is best used in loose soils, where the 'point' will usually fill when the dibber is withdrawn from the soil.

Trowel: another useful tool for lifting young plants so that they can be removed with a ball of earth attached to their roots. It is also useful for planting, and here you should make sure that the holes are large enough to take the roots without cramping.

Introduction

Garden line: this is needed to mark out straight drills and rows. Use a good length of some stout binder twine, or string that will not rot. Fix this to two sticks.

These are the main tools, but, of course, there are many others: wheelbarrow, hose, watering can and sprayer. Also, if you have to deal with rough ground, you may need a bill or swap hook and a scythe, shears for trimming hedges and secateurs.

There is one vital rule which applies to all tools, and that is—keep them clean and carefully stored when not in use. This isn't unnecessary fussiness, the tools actually work better and are easier to use if they are in good condition.

The Land, Soils and Digging

It is likely, if you are a new gardener, that the plot you are intending to cultivate will be in bad condition, probably overgrown, and possibly never used for vegetables before. So your first task is to clear and prepare the land. Don't despair if this seems an impossible task. Work through it slowly, bit by bit. Once you have a workable section under control, you can begin to make use of it, by sowing and planting your first crops. Then as you work through the rest of the plot, the sight of growing crops will give you extra encouragement to carry on with the heavy work.

As I said earlier, there is no real beginning or end to the gardener's year. You can start your clearing and digging at any time, so long as the weather is not against you. After a few months you will be able to fit your work into the monthly plan.

Soils

It is important to assess the condition and character of your soil at the very start, as this will determine what you do and what crops you can grow. Few vegetable patches have 'a perfect soil' to begin with, but most soils can be made useful and fertile after a while. The perfect soil is a good loam, which is 'fertile soil consisting of clay and sand, together with humus (decayed animal and vegetable matter)'. If there is more sand than clay, the soil is light, whereas more clay makes the soil heavy. Generally these loams are easy to work and are suitable for most crops.

But to begin with, your soil may be far from this ideal. The main problems you are likely to encounter are heavy clay, chalk, sand, a rocky or very heavy subsoil, stones and dust. But, given time, all these can be dealt with so that the soil is workable—if not perfect.

Heavy clay

This needs deep digging and plenty of stable manure, compost, leaf-mould or wood ash—anything that will make the soil fertile. Dig these soils early in the winter, and leave them in ridges so that the clods can be weathered; in the spring they can be broken down with a fork. After a while the soil will be workable, although it will always be fairly heavy; but clay will hold moisture much better than some lighter soils. Most crops can be grown except long roots like carrots and parsnips, although even these can be successful if special holes are made for the roots.

Chalk

The presence of chalk means that the soil is alkaline, so it does not need to be limed. Vegetables such as brassicas thrive in the light, shallow soil, although there is always a danger of drought as chalk soil drains very fast. This can be improved by first breaking up the subsoil to help root penetration, then mulching the surface with rotted grass cuttings or peat to retain moisture.

Introduction

Sand

The problem with sand is that it loses moisture very quickly, so you need to add decaying vegetation or some other substance that will hold moisture in the soil. Generally these very sandy soils can be dug much later than heavy clay soils; they do not need weathering.

Heavy subsoil

If you are deep digging, you may find that there is an impassable layer of chalk, flints or gravel a few inches below the good topsoil. This can be dealt with: the important point is to avoid bringing this subsoil to the surface. Break it up, with a pick if necessary, and pack it with manure, leaves, etc. This will stop fast drainage from the topsoil and give the crops some extra nutrients. These shallow soils are not much good for long-rooted varieties of carrots, parsnips, etc. Grow the stump-rooted varieties instead.

Stones

These are quite easily dealt with. Raking is the best way of clearing large stones from the surface of the soil. But a few stones will help drainage, so don't be too thorough, particularly below the surface.

Dust

Although not widespread, dust is a real menace in some areas, particularly East Anglia. It is very light soil, which can produce dust storms in high winds, and needs to be made rich and heavy. Add quantities of manure, chopped turf, etc. and dig them well into the soil; they are no use if simply forked around on the surface. However, when crops are growing you can spread the surface with wet leaf-mould or strawy manure as an added protection.

Lime

A good soil must have humus and lime present in the right proportions. If you have too much humus, the soil becomes acid and sour, and will need extra lime to restore the balance and reduce the acidity. This is often the case with neglected town gardens where so-called 'black soil' is produced which is full of humus but almost entirely lacking in lime.

You should not add lime to chalk soils or to soils that appear very alkaline if you check them with a soil-testing kit. If you decide that the soil does need lime, the best method is to treat one-third of your plot each year, starting with the area used for brassicas. Each section then has a dressing every three years.

Use powdered limestone or chalk and add 6-8oz per sq yd. Fork it lightly into the soil during the winter, but not at the same time as manure, since the two will react together. You may need to add extra lime if you know that there is a tendency to produce club root in brassicas, or if your climate is very wet. In these cases you should add lime each year.

Digging

I don't intend to give a long account of the merits and technicalities of digging. It is in no way as mysterious as some gardeners would have us believe. Successful digging can be achieved by sticking to a few basic rules:

(i) Go steadily and be thorough. If you rush digging you will not only wear yourself out—unless you are really fit—but you will also need to repeat your work sooner than you think.
(ii) Use the right tool for the job. In most cases a spade is best, except in heavy clay soils where a fork is more useful for breaking up the soil. Keep the spade or fork clean while you are digging. It may become caked with earth and feel as heavy as lead if it isn't scraped occasionally.

(iii) Handle the tool correctly. Dig as deeply as possible with the spade pushed vertically into the soil.

(iv) Organize your digging. This may mean dividing your plot into sections, depending on its size. Mark each section with a line, and concentrate on clearing one section at a time, using the rest for bonfires, etc. Organization will save you time and effort, so keep to straight rows, evenly dug so that the overall surface is level.

There are really three main types of digging: single digging, one spit deep; double digging cultivated land; double digging rough grassland.

Single digging

(i) Open up a trench at the top end of the plot, one spit deep and 1ft wide; take the soil to the other end in a barrow, ready to fill the final trench.

(ii) Work from left to right along the row, cutting off each spit at right angles to the trench before actually digging.

(iii) Dig a full spit, with the spade vertical, and turn the soil into the first trench.

(iv) If you are adding manure put this into the bottom of the trench before covering with soil.

(v) Continue to dig and fill trenches until you reach the end of the plot. Fill the last trench with the soil barrowed from the top end.

Double digging

(i) Open up a trench as before, except make it 2ft wide and one spit deep. Barrow the soil to the other end of the plot.

(ii) Break up the soil in the bottom of the trench to the full depth of a fork.

(iii) Mark out a second trench the same width; dig this to one spit with the spade and transfer the soil into the first trench.

(iv) Break up the soil at the bottom of this second trench and transfer the 'crumbs' to the first trench.

(v) When you add manure, fork it into the bottom of each trench as you proceed.

Double digging grassland

(i) Skim off a 2ft width of the earth and grass to a depth of 2″ and move the turf to the other end of the plot; take out a trench 2ft wide as before, and similarly barrow to the end of the plot.

(ii) Skim turf from a second trench and put into the first trench, upside down and chopped into small pieces.

(iii) Cover with soil from the second trench and then transfer 'crumbs' from the bottom of the second trench into the first.

(iv) Proceed along the plot as above, finishing with the turf and soil from the first trench which are used to fill the last trench that you dig out.

Seeds, Crops and the Cropping Plan

Once you have started to get your plot in order, you will need to think about the crops you want to grow, and also some sort of layout for the ground. Both of these will depend on the size of your plot, the climate, the soil and so on. You should try to get a balanced selection of crops which will provide you with food throughout the whole year. If you have plenty of space, you can grow a great many different vegetables, but the final choice will depend on what you like to eat. But you should also aim to make the most profitable use of the ground.

Rotation of crops

Rotation is the basis on which the layout of a vegetable garden depends. It means that crops are grown on different ground each year. There are many reasons for this approach. First, the natural control of pests and diseases. Most of these are specific—such as

Introduction wireworm in potatoes, or onion fly. They can completely ruin a crop if it is to their liking, so if a crop is replaced each year with something else that the pests do not attack, vegetables if properly tended will remain generally healthy, and a build up of the pest or disease will be controlled. The same applies to diseases like club root on cabbages. Rotation is a simple way of controlling and limiting the effects of pests and diseases.

Then there are the actual food requirements of the crops themselves. For instance the brassicas use up a lot of lime, whereas potatoes tend to take potash from the soil. If the crops were grown in the same spot each year, the soil would soon be depleted, and those crops would fail. By rotating the crops in a certain order, they can always be grown in soil that is fertile and contains sufficient of their specific requirements.

Finally there is soil depth. Plants like brassicas, which have a short root system, only take food from the surface of the soil, leaving the lower depths still rich; if long-rooted crops are grown after them, they can take further nourishment from this soil.

A Simple Cropping Plan

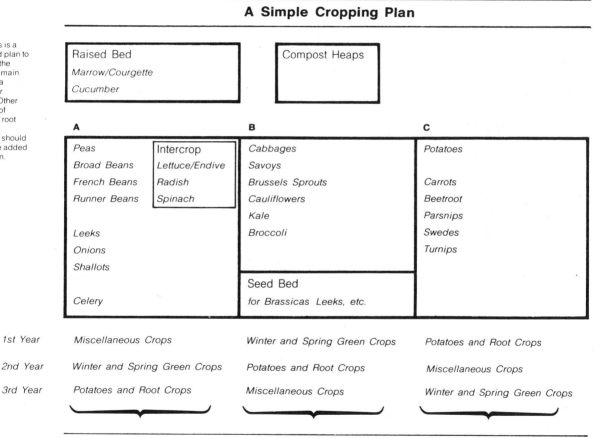

Note: This is a simplified plan to illustrate the layout for main crops on a three-year rotation. Other varieties of greens or root crops, for example, should simply be added to the plan.

A		B	C
Peas	Intercrop	Cabbages	Potatoes
Broad Beans	Lettuce/Endive	Savoys	
French Beans	Radish	Brussels Sprouts	Carrots
Runner Beans	Spinach	Cauliflowers	Beetroot
		Kale	Parsnips
Leeks		Broccoli	Swedes
Onions			Turnips
Shallots			
		Seed Bed	
Celery		for Brassicas Leeks, etc.	

	A	B	C
1st Year	Miscellaneous Crops	Winter and Spring Green Crops	Potatoes and Root Crops
2nd Year	Winter and Spring Green Crops	Potatoes and Root Crops	Miscellaneous Crops
3rd Year	Potatoes and Root Crops	Miscellaneous Crops	Winter and Spring Green Crops

On a normal plot or allotment, the easiest way of organizing the cropping plan is to divide the plot into three sections and to rotate each year, as shown on the plan, so a crop is only grown in the same spot every three years. You will see that the crops are divided up into the following sections:

(a) Miscellaneous—including legumes, onions, etc.
(b) Winter and spring green crops
(c) Potatoes and root crops

These three sections should be treated differently as regards manuring, etc.

(a) Need a rich soil, plenty of manure,

15

compost and leaf mould.

(b) This should be the first section that you lime. Also a small amount of general fertilizer will help growth.

(c) Fresh manure should not be applied on this section. However, if it has been under cultivation for several years it will need little treatment except deep digging. Bone meal—or a phosphate fertilizer used sparingly—will help the root crops.

Rotate the crops each year as shown on the plan and treat each section as listed above.*

You may also want to include some 'permanent' crops like rhubarb and asparagus in your garden. These, naturally enough, aren't included in the rotation. The other point to notice on the plan is 'intercropping'. This is a system whereby quick-growing crops like radishes and spinach are planted between rows of slow-growing crops like legumes and brassicas. There are two main reasons for this. Firstly it is a way of using up space, and secondly the conditions between these rows suit crops like radishes and spinach—the soil is rich and moist, and there is plenty of shade.

Choice of seeds

This is really a matter of personal taste. You can grow what you like, but try to balance the food value and taste of the crops with economy and the best use of the land. There is one rule: don't try to grow too much. Crops must have plenty of space to grow and develop properly; if you sow too thickly or plant rows too close together, the plants have to compete desperately for the limited amount of food, moisture and light, and the result is a succession of poor crops.

The choice I have made is a quite

*Three-year rotation plans can be worked out to scale to suit individual needs on the squared pages at the end of this book.

straightforward one. I have intentionally avoided many 'exotic' vegetables for several reasons. They require, on the whole, more specialist growing techniques than normal crops, and they need, in most cases, artificial heat in their early stages—this means a greenhouse or heated frame—and to thrive, they need reliable weather. Also they cannot be fitted into an overall yearly plan. But this doesn't mean that you shouldn't try to grow them—there are plenty to choose from: aubergines, green peppers, asparagus pea, mangetout, cardoons, Chinese cabbage, etc. There is a great deal of information about growing them in Brian Furner's book *Less Usual Vegetables* (Macdonald & Jane's).

You may need to adapt my list slightly, depending on where you live. Gardeners in the north, for example, will probably not be able to grow outdoor tomatoes, sweet corn, perhaps even runner beans, and might want to replace these with summer cauliflowers and cabbages.

Once you have decided what crops you want to grow, then it is time to consult the seed catalogues to see what varieties are available. It is best to stick to the reputable names—Suttons, Thompson & Morgan, Carters or Dobies unless you find an unusually good local supplier. Some enquiries at the local gardening shop or ironmonger's will help.

The following chart lists all the crops mentioned in detail in the calendar. You can refer to it whenever you want to know when to plant, and then look in the monthly sections for more information.

The sowing and planting dates given on the chart generally apply to southern regions of the country. If you live in the north, where the growing season tends to be later and shorter, you will need to adjust your schedule. The important thing is to understand your local climate; if it is colder than average, you will need to delay sowing by a week or two. This is usually the case in the north. But if you live in a particularly warm, sheltered spot, you may be able to bring forward your work by a week or so.

Pelleted seeds
A great many vegetable seeds are now available in pellet form, that is with a protective coating which slowly breaks down in the soil. There are advantages and disadvantages. The seeds are quite expensive, and, because of the coating, they take longer to germinate. It is also even more important to keep the soil moist after sowing, otherwise the seeds may not germinate at all. On the other hand, the coating gives protection to the seeds themselves, and the extra cost can be balanced against the more accurate and less wasteful sowing of these large 'seeds'. They can also be spaced evenly so that thinning is much easier.

Crop	Sowing	Planting out	When ready	Available until (s = crops in store)
Artichoke, Globe	—	April	June	August
Artichoke, Jerusalem	—	February	November	March (s)
Asparagus	—	March	May	June
Bean, Broad	Feb.-May	—	June	August
Bean, French	May	—	July	September
Bean, Runner	May-June	—	July	October
Beetroot	April	—	July	March (s)
Broccoli, Sprouting	March-May	May-July	October	April
Brussels Sprouts	March	May-June	November	March
Cabbage, spring	August	October	March	June
Cabbage, winter	March	May	October	January
Cabbage, red	April	June	November	January
Carrot	March-April	—	June	March (s)
Cauliflower	April	June	July	October
Celeriac	April	June	October	March (s)
Celery	April (unreliable)	June	November	March
Cucumber	May	—	August	October
Endive	June-August	—	October—through the winter	
Garlic	March	—	July	March (s)

17

Introduction

Crop	Sowing	Planting Out	When ready	Available until (s = crops in store)
Kale, winter	April	June	December onwards	
spring	July	—	April onwards	
Kohl-rabi, early	April	—	July onwards	
late	July	—	October	March (s)
Leek	March	July	October	April
Lettuce	March–Aug.	Ready 10 weeks after sowing		
Marrow	May	—	August	Jan (s)
Onion	March	—	September	April (s)
	August	—	June	September (s)
Parsnip	March	—	November	March (s)
Pea, early	March	—	June	July
maincrop	April	—	July	August
Potato, early	March–April	—	July	August
maincrop	April–May	—	September	April (s)
Radish, summer	April–Aug.	Ready 5–6 weeks after sowing		
winter	Aug.–Oct.	Ready 8 weeks after sowing		
Rhubarb	—	February	April	July
Salsify	April	—	October	March (s)
Scorzonera	April	—	October	March (s)
Shallot	February	—	July	March (s)
Spinach, summer	Feb.–May	—	May	September
perpetual	July	—	Sept. onwards	
Swede	June	—	December	April (s)
Sweet Corn	May	—	August	September
Tomato	—	June	August	October
Turnip, early	March	—	June onwards	
late	August	—	November	March (s)

The importance of varieties

Varieties—or to give them their correct name, cultivars—tend to change through the years. Old-established names are replaced by new cross-breeds or hybrids. This is part of the business of agriculture. But today there are signs of another trend, that of levelling. There is tremendous economic and political pressure to re-organize the food we eat, and part of this official policy is the reduction, and even elimination, of certain varieties of vegetables.

Consider the potato, for example. It is not simply 'a potato'. It has a name, a

18

Introduction special taste, and texture; it may be floury or soapy, pure white or almost yellow in colour. There are some varieties which are perfect for baking in their skins; others make good chips and so on. All these possibilities, all these varieties need to be kept.

The trend of levelling is already well-known in other areas of food and drink—you have only to buy a loaf of bread to realize that. We must fight this wherever we find it. In the case of vegetables that means learning about different varieties, understanding their different uses, growing them and eating them. And we should *demand* them in shops and markets.

A list of varieties

In the following list, I have given a selection of useful varieties for various crops. If a particular crop is not mentioned, then the choice of variety is not important, as far as growing is concerned.

Globe Artichoke: *Vert de Laon.* This variety can only be bought as offsets.
Asparagus: *Connover's Colossal.* Either as seeds or root clumps.
Broad Bean: spring sowing—*Green Longpod/Green Windsor.*
autumn sowing—*Aquadulce/Seville Longpod.*
Dwarf French Beans: *Masterpiece/ Tendergreen/The Prince.*
Runner Beans: climbing—*Achievement/Enorma/Prizewinner.*
dwarf—*Hammond's Dwarf Scarlet.*
Beetroot: round, April sowing—*Crimson Globe.*
round, July sowing—*Little Ball.*
long—*Cheltenham Green Top.*
Broccoli (winter cauliflower): January/February—*Adam's Early White.*
April—*St. George.*
Brussels Sprouts: *Peer Gynt/Sigmund.*
Cabbage: spring sown for summer use—*Babyhead* (small round

head)/*Hispi* (small pointed head)/*Golden Acre* (large round head).
summer sown for winter use—*Drumhead/Winter Monarch/January King/Winnigstadt* (pointed head).
autumn sown for spring use—*Harbinger/Wheeler's Imperial* (both small)/*Durham Early/Offenham.*
white cabbage for storing—*Holland Winter White.*
Carrot: long rooted—*New Red Intermediate.*
others—*Autumn King/Chantenay.*
Cauliflower: summer cutting—*Alpha/All The Year Round/Delta.*
autumn cutting—*Canberra/ Dominant/South Pacific.*
Celeriac: *Globus.*
Celery: trench—*Giant White/Giant Red.*
self-blanching—*Golden Self Blanching/Avonpearl/Greensnap.*
Cucumber: ridge—*Burpless/Burpee Hybrid.*
Endive: autumn—*Green Curled.*
winter—*Batavian Broad-leaved.*
Kale: *Dwarf Curled/Hungry Gap* (late sowing, does not need transplanting).
Leek: maincrop—*Musselburgh.*
Lettuce: summer cabbage—*Buttercrunch/Cobham Green/Mildura/Webb's Wonderful* (crisp, curled).
summer cos—*Little Gem/Lobjoit's Green.*
winter cabbage—*Winter Imperial/Winter Crop.*
winter cos—*Winter Density.*
Marrow: bush—*Green Bush/White Bush.*
trailing—*Long Green Trailing.*
Onion: sets—*Rijnsburger/Stuttgarter Riesen.*
spring sown seeds—*Bedfordshire Champion/Giant Zittau.*
autumn sown seeds—*Reliance/Solidity.*
for salads—*White Lisbon.*
for pickling—*Small Paris Silverskin.*
Parsnip: short—*Avonresister/Offenham

long—*Lisbonnais/Tender and True.*
Pea: early—*Feltham First/Kelvedon Wonder* (both 1½-2ft).
maincrop—*Achievement* (4½ft)/*Lincoln* (2ft).
Potato: early—*Duke of York/Epicure/Arran Pilot/Ulster Chieftain.*
maincrop—*Desiree/King Edward/Majestic/Pentland Crown.*
Radish: round— *Cherry Belle/Scarlet Globe.*
long—*French Breakfast.*
winter—*Black Spanish/Chinese Rose.*
Rhubarb: early—*Timperley Early* (crowns only).
maincrop—*Cawood Castle* (crowns only).
Spinach: round-seeded—*King of Denmark/Long Standing Round.*
beet (perpetual)—*New Zealand.*
prickly—*Giant Leaved Prickly.*
Swede: Any purple topped variety.
Sweet Corn: early—*Canada Cross/Earliking.*
mid-season—*North Star.*
Tomatoes: outdoor—*Harbinger/ Gardener's Delight/Market King.*
outdoor bush—*Sleaford Abundance.*
Turnips: early round roots—*Snowball.*
early flat-rounded roots—*Purple Milan/White Milan.*
maincrop, round roots—*Golden Ball/Green-Top Stone.*

Pests, Diseases and Predators

It is a fact of gardening life that pests and diseases have to be dealt with. The essential point is to use a method that is safe and efficient. Chemical sprays and pesticides can be harmful to plant life, to birds, to harmless insects, and to us. They should be used only in an emergency, when all other methods have failed. The alternatives are often very unusual, they may involve more time and work, but they are safe, specific and usually quite cheap.

Eradication of pests involves consideration of every aspect of garden ecology; a very complex and delicately balanced system of micro-organisms, fungi, insects, birds and animals. If you upset this balance, even slightly, the effect on the life of the garden can be quite considerable. The first problem is to be able to distinguish between friends and enemies. Insects, for instance, are not universally 'the enemy': they pollinate plants, they prey on other insects, they work in the soil, aerating it and breaking down organic matter. In fact, they are vital to the garden. Any measures against insect pests, therefore, must be specific, dealing efficiently with harmful insects without any repercussions on others essential to the well-being of the garden. So, get to know your allies—the ladybirds, spiders, red ants and so on.

Birds can be a real nuisance in the vegetable garden, though they prey on many harmful insects and grubs. However, they can be discouraged fairly easily with the use of wire or plastic netting, cloches, strands of black cotton and so on. Mice and rabbits are the worst offenders from the animal world and they are most efficiently kept down by a terrier or cat, but that is a rather long term investment.

I have not attempted more than a summary of the various aspects of pest control in the garden, but I have tried to present some idea of the importance of maintaining the natural balance, of distinguishing between the useful and the destructive, and how much pest control can be achieved by encouraging some creatures while discouraging others. There is another relationship to be considered—that between the soil and pests. A poor infertile soil will often encourage pests. And infestation can be an important warning sign that the soil needs replenishing. Often when we deal with pests we are only treating symptoms rather than causes.

An American entomologist has observed that 'more pests can be controlled in front of a February fire with a garden notebook and a seed catalogue than can ever be knocked out in hand-to-hand combat in the garden'. This is good advice. You should plan carefully, work out an effective system of crop rotation, check your notes to see if it is worth persisting with crops that become infested every year, aim to plant and sow at the right time, try out different varieties, and keep your soil cultivated.

Finally, if all other methods fail, you may feel that a chemical spray is your last chance of eradicating a pest. Use it carefully 'like a stiletto rather than a scythe'. Care, accuracy and thoughtfulness are the key words.

Now for specific pests and specific remedies. I have listed here all the common sources of trouble in the vegetable garden, but for more information you should read the publications put out by the Henry Doubleday Association and study *Gardening without Poisons* by Beatrice Trum Hunter (Hamish Hamilton 1965).

Pests

Aphids: Blackfly. This attacks broad beans, and occasionally French beans and spinach. You can anticipate attack by planting early, and by nipping out the tender tops of the plants once they are in flower. If the crops are attacked, you should also spray with a soap solution (see p. 57).

Greenfly. This attacks all varieties of brassicas. Spraying with a soap solution is the best method of dealing with them.

Beetles: Turnip flea beetle. This attacks young turnips and also brassicas by nibbling the leaves. Dust the plants with old soot; it must be old or

it will scorch the leaves. A dusting with *plain* Derris powder is also effective, but remember to keep this well away from fish ponds as it was originally used as a fish poison.

Caterpillars: These are the soft larvae of butterflies and moths. The common ones in the vegetable garden are the green or grey cabbage moth and butterfly caterpillars, yellow pea moth caterpillars that feed on the pods, the large swift moth caterpillars which are white and live in the soil, and cutworms which are fat and brown, and attack root vegetables such as carrots and beetroot. The soil caterpillars can be controlled by regular digging and by keeping down weeds. The others, which live on leaves and stalks can be picked off by hand. You can also dust with Derris powder. Always check the underside of the leaves.

Eelworms: These affect mainly potatoes and onions in the vegetable garden. They cause yellowing of the leaves and stunted growth. There is no really effective treatment. All you can do is to rotate your crops, leaving the affected ground clear for 3 years. With potatoes you can try growing varieties like early Pentland Meteor, or maincrop Maris Piper, which have some resistance to eelworm attack.

Flies: Cabbage root fly. This attacks young brassicas and also some root crops such as turnips and swedes. The plants begin to wilt and turn a yellow-blue colour. You can hoe some naphthalene along the rows when you plant the cabbages, or you can fit 6″ squares of roofing felt round the stem of each plant as a kind of collar which sits on the surface and stops the eggs entering the soil around the roots. Yoghurt cartons have also been tried for this kind of protection.

Carrot fly. The greatest danger comes

Introduction

during thinning, since the carrot fly is attracted by scent. It lays its eggs around the surface of the soil and the larvae attack the roots. Be careful when you are thinning; firm the soil around the remaining plants; destroy all leaves; put down either some naphthalene or sand soaked in paraffin along the rows to mask the scent. Strong smelling herbs can also be grown between the rows for this purpose.

Onion fly. The plants wilt and eventually rot when infected. Treat the problem as for carrot fly, and change the site for onions next year if the crop has been infested. Onions grown from sets are less likely to be attacked.

Slugs: There are some easy methods of dealing with these creatures. One way is to trap them using old pots or boards, hollowed out grapefruit, etc. under which the slugs hide. These traps can be checked each day and the slugs collected and disposed of. Another method is to sink a small pot or shallow dish into the soil and fill it with equal parts of beer and water, flavoured with sugar. You will need to set up quite a number of traps to deal effectively with slugs. Also a little salt or lime scattered in the right places will deter them.

Wireworms: These grubs burrow into root crops and can be trapped by sinking pieces of carrot into the ground, attached to sticks. The wireworms burrow and feed on these bits of bait which can be removed periodically, along with the catch of worms. Potatoes are often ruined by wireworm if they are left in the soil too long after the foliage has died.

Diseases

Celery heart rot: This occurs mainly in wet weather, or if the crop has been watered carelessly. There is no effective treatment, but the risk of disease can be minimised if you handle the plants carefully, so that they are not wounded in any way, and also water them accurately.

Brassica club root: There are several ways of controlling this fungus that forms bulbous growths on the roots, but it is impossible to eradicate it completely. The first essential is to maintain healthy soil and it should be well limed. Another preventive measure is to drop small pieces of rhubarb into the planting holes. You should also keep down cruciferous weeds like shepherd's purse, on which the disease over-winters.

Potato blight: You can minimise the chance of this by growing a blight resistant variety—check the catalogues for a suitable choice. If blight does attack, cut off all the foliage and burn it straight away; then wait a couple of weeks before lifting the potatoes, and make sure you do not leave any in the ground, as blight spores will over-winter on them and reappear next season.

Potato scab: The spots and blemishes caused by this disease are a nuisance. But a balanced soil, with plenty of organic matter will discourage the fungus which produces scab.

Manure and the Compost Heap

The main point of adding manure to the soil is to replace essential foods needed by crops as well as to supply humus. In this book I have concentrated on the use of organic manures and enrichers; this is the way I work in the garden, and it is a good system. Of course it may be necessary to add some chemical fertilisers if the ground is in very bad condition, but their indiscriminate use can change the composition of the soil quite radically, particularly if organic matter is not added as well.

This system naturally makes some special demands on the gardener. The main problem is obtaining a source of supply. Compost, leaf mould, grass cuttings, etc. can be salvaged from the garden itself, but farmyard manure has to be bought. It is becoming simpler to get hold of this nowadays: farmers and horse owners advertise in the newspapers, they put up signs along the roadside; they may even deliver the stuff for you for a small extra charge.

If you are unable to get manure, for one reason or another, you can overcome this by 'green manuring'. This involves growing a green crop at the beginning or towards the end of the growing season; these crops are then dug into the soil. The method is quite simple: clear and rake over the ground and then broadcast seeds of either mustard, rape or Italian ryegrass (1 oz per sq yd) and rake them in. Once the plants are about 1 ft tall, they can be dug into the soil. It is also possible to grow comfrey for green manure. This was developed by Lawrence Hills of the Henry Doubleday Research Association, Convent Lane, Bocking, Braintree, Essex. Hills has probably done more than anyone to promote organic gardening in recent years. It is worth getting in touch with the Association if you are interested in this system of gardening. They have also done a great deal of work on controlling pests and diseases without resorting to chemicals (see pp. 20-22).

Horse manure

If this is mixed with straw it is excellent for heavy ground as it helps to break up the soil. Dig it into heavy soils before Christmas, and into light soils in the early spring. It must not be put on to ground used for growing root crops, or brassicas that stand through the winter. Usual rate quoted is 1 bucketful per sq yd

Cow and pig manure

Both of these are useful on lighter soils as they help to retain moisture; on heavy soil they are not effective. Apply them at the same rate as horse manure.

Chicken manure

This is very powerful stuff, and it should be mixed with an equal amount of soil after it has been collected. An occasional trowelful of this mixture can be hoed in around growing crops.

Vegetable refuse

This includes coarse weeds, old greenstuff, vegetable peelings and leaves. The refuse can be dug in wherever it is needed, but make sure it is buried well below the surface of the soil.

Spent hops

If you can get hold of spent hops from a brewery, this can be dug in like stable manure and is a good source of humus.

Seaweed

Another useful substance, if you can get hold of it. It provides humus and potash—so it is good for many crops, e.g. potatoes and asparagus. Dig it deeply into the soil in the winter.

Wood ash

Not a manure, but it is a useful source of potash for root crops. It should be forked into the surface soil before planting—a trowelful per sq yd. The residue of wood ash is one of the advantages of having bonfires. Keep it dry until you need it, and be very sparing if your soil is light, as wood ash will make it still lighter.

Liquid Manure

This is useful once plants are established. It can be easily made by suspending a sack of coarse manure in a barrel of water for a couple of days.

The useful constituents dissolve in the water, and can then be watered on to the soil. You must, however, dilute the liquid manure with an equal quantity of water before you use it on crops like tomatoes, beans and onions.

Mulching

This involves top dressing the soil around crops with a thick layer of organic matter, which helps to retain moisture—especially during a dry growing season. It also keeps the plants cool, supplies extra nutrients and helps to keep down weeds.

The best mulching materials are old leaf mould, decayed grass cuttings and peat. With grass cuttings it is essential that they have been allowed to rot in a heap for at least a year; never put fresh cuttings onto the land. Peat should be thoroughly wet before it is used as a mulch, particularly if it has been bought as a dry compressed bale.

If the soil is dry you should always water it well before spreading any sort of mulch.

The Compost Heap

This is an essential feature of the vegetable garden. All old greenstuff, leaves, etc. can be put onto the heap and allowed to rot. When it is ready the compost can be dug into the ground. The heap is built up in layers. Begin with a layer of leaves and then continue with layers of heavier refuse, more leaves and so on. It may be worth including several thin layers of soil and manure to enrich the heap and to make it bulky. The heap should be kept moist to encourage decomposition, and may need watering from time to time. It should also be kept under control—neat and compressed. When it has reached a suitable height (about 4 ft) it can be turned over and covered with a layer of soil. If the heap is started in January, it should be ready for turning in late summer, and finally ready for use when winter digging begins.

Preserving, Storing and the Deep Freeze

Preserving is a big subject and it is outside the scope of this book, but it is an essential part of food gardening, and I would refer readers to my book *Jams, Pickles and Chutneys* (Macmillan and Penguin) in which I deal with preserving, drying and storing in detail. The only point I want to stress here is the importance of planning for preserves just as much as you plan for fresh vegetables, and be sure to make full use of the different methods if you have a glut of any crops. There is hardly a vegetable that cannot be transformed into some kind of preserve. I have, however, given quite a number of suggestions throughout this book.

The same applies to storing, although I have dealt with this in much more detail, because it is in a sense much nearer to the gardening aspect of food than true preserving. Most methods of storing are quite straightforward, and I have mentioned them in the calendar. One method, however, does need some description, and that is the clamp.

To build a clamp

This is basically a heap of root crops protected with straw or soil for winter storage. It is mainly used for potatoes, carrots and beetroot.

You can construct a clamp for potatoes as follows:

(1) Choose a dry spot outside, spread a 2in layer of ashes and cover this with a layer of straw.
(2) Heap the potatoes on to this straw

base, making as neat a pile as possible, with sloping sides.

(3) Cover the potatoes with another layer of straw and leave them to 'sweat' for a few days.

(4) Then cover completely with a 3in layer of soil, made firm and smooth with the back of a spade, so that the potatoes are completely enclosed. All sides of the clamp should slope, so that rain is easily directed off it. The soil can be taken from around the clamp itself, thus leaving a trench into which rain water can run.

Beetroot and carrots can be clamped in a slightly different way. They are stored between layers of ashes. Start with a 2in layer of ashes, then a single layer of roots, arranged like spokes in a wheel, cover them with another 2in layer of ashes and so on. Decrease the circumference of the clamp as it gets higher to form a conical structure. Cover the clamp with a 3in layer of straw and put a ventilator in by making a twisted bundle of straw, and setting it into the top of the clamp.

Don't forget to replace any part of the wall of the clamp that is disturbed when you take out roots for the kitchen.

The deep freeze

I have never been totally convinced about the value of the deep freeze, particularly with regard to vegetables, as I have never tasted a frozen vegetable—including the well-known pea—which could match a fresh vegetable of any sort. There is a widespread claim that the freezer liberates the cook; any dish can be cooked at any time of the year when seasonal vegetables are no longer available. I do not believe in this. The cook, like the gardener, has to live and work *with* the seasons. If food is a fundamental part of your life, whatever your circumstances, the real pleasure comes from seasonal crops. This becomes even more important once you start growing your own food. Many 'freezer-cooks' want to have summer vegetables throughout the year; they wish to forget winter. But I maintain there is more taste and pleasure in fresh swedes and turnips than in any packet of soggy runner beans.

There is also the argument that gluts and surplus vegetables can be fully used up. This really amounts to proper planning and growing sufficient for your needs. A freezer can be useful if you have grown more of one crop than you immediately need, for you can freeze the surplus. If you are simply feeding your family through the year, however, it only takes a little skill and experience to sow approximately the right quantities of different vegetables to give you fresh vegetables all the year round.

This leads on to preserving. A deep freeze doesn't preserve, it stores. The best you can hope for is that the food will return to a near fresh state when thawed. Preserving—that is pickling, salting, jam and chutney making—transforms the food into something entirely new, with a whole range of different flavours and textures. If you have a freezer, don't entirely forget about preserving surplus food. Use the two methods together, and handle the freezer sensibly when it is necessary. Don't use it as a dustbin.

JANUARY

"What greater crime
than a loss of time."

Deepest winter. Even so, there are jobs still to be done. The weather may be cold or freezing, but at every possible moment you must go out into the garden. Time now to prepare the land for spring sowings and summer crops—and this means digging, manuring and cleaning up the ground.

When the weather is impossible, give a little time indoors to planning. Decide what you want to grow, check the seed catalogues, and order your seeds in plenty of time. And draw a plan, but make sure you allow plenty of space for your crops; there is no virtue and no profit in cramming row against row.

A food garden should always be producing and working for you; it should never be fallow or resting. So, even in bleak January you should be able to lift leeks, parsnips, Jerusalem artichokes and celery—all crops that can be 'stored' in the soil.

After Christmas, when perhaps your enthusiasm begins to fail, have a look and see what you have achieved and produced throughout the past year. If your garden is still providing you with food—either fresh or from stores —then it is working well. If not, then this is a good time to change your plans. It may be that a little reorganization of crops is all that is needed. Above all, don't be discouraged if your garden *is* barren; that is your challenge for the coming year.

January

Summary

1) *Heavy work: digging and manuring, lime, clearing and compost, the marrow bed.*

2) *Planning: a cropping plan, choosing seeds, seed potatoes.*

3) *Crops in the soil: Jerusalem artichokes, parsnips, leeks, celery.*

4) *Fresh pickings: brussels sprouts, cabbages and other brassicas.*

5) *Stores: potatoes, root crops, shallots.*

Heavy Work

Digging and manuring

Keep digging. This is work for days when the weather is good. It is unlikely that all the digging, manuring and clearing will be completed before Christmas, particularly if you have leeks and other crops in the soil, but you must aim to have nearly all the work finished by the end of this month. When you are digging at this time of year, it is best to throw up the soil in ridges; this gives the weather a chance to work on it and break down the clods.

As you eat and use up rows of standing crops, dig through and clear the land and add manure (see pages 22-23). You should try to add manure early on heavy soil, and later on well-drained, light soil; this stops the goodness being washed away by winter rain.

If you are extending your plot you should also aim to have all the new ground ready by the end of the month.

Lime

If your soil needs lime (see page 13) make sure you add this at the right time. Never mix lime and manure together as they react together, and the value of both is lost. If you add manure in the autumn or any time before Christmas, add lime over the next few weeks, and vice versa.

Use powdered limestone or chalk and spread 6-8oz. per sq. yd. Simply fork it in lightly; don't leave it on the surface of the soil or dig it in too deep.

Clearing and compost

It is worth spending some time clearing and tidying up the garden generally—sweeping paths, raking up leaves, collecting dead wood and so on. Leaves can be put into a heap and kept

A compost heap is built up over several months using leaves, rotted greenstuff and garden refuse in rough layers. Depending on conditions, it will be matured in two to three months after completion.

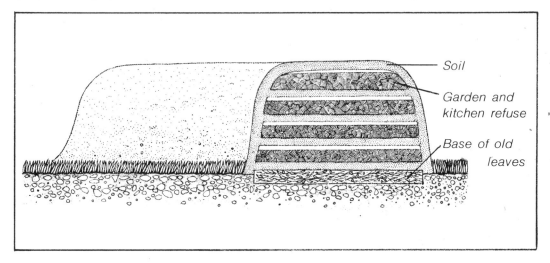

Soil

Garden and kitchen refuse

Base of old leaves

for leaf-mould, or they can be used to start or interlayer a compost heap. Most of last year's compost will be in the soil by now, so you should begin to build a new heap (see p. 24). Dead wood can either be taken indoors for your fire, or burned outside, and the ash collected and stored for use later in the year.

The marrow bed

If you decide to grow marrows, it is best to start the marrow bed early. This is really a very compressed compost heap, which can be built up from well-rotted manure and other refuse. This is covered later in the year with about 3in of good soil.

Planning

A Cropping Plan

During the month, when the weather is bad, or in the evenings when you have some spare time, draw up a cropping plan similar to the one given earlier (see p. 15). The important point here is to organize some sort of crop rotation. If this is your first year, simply measure out your plot and divide it into three main sections:

(a) miscellaneous crops, e.g. legumes, onions
(b) winter and spring green crops
(c) potatoes and root crops

These three sections should be treated differently when it comes to adding manure or fertilizers (see pp. 15-16). To ensure that you don't make any mistakes, keep a notebook showing precisely how you have organized your plot. This record doesn't have to be too formal, simply an account of how your garden is progressing.

Later in the year it is worth recording when you plant crops, when the first pickings are made and how much food each crop produces. Apart from anything else, this is concrete evidence of the value of the garden; it will justify your work and keep your enthusiasm going. Keeping records will teach you to watch your garden with a keen eye, to note down changes in the weather, or the first sighting of pest damage. By the end of the year you should have a complete picture of all that has happened in your garden.

People who have established gardens should simply arrange a rotation of their crops for the coming year and should have a good look at their notebooks. What crops did best last year? Why did others fail? Is it worth growing them, perhaps in a different position? Is there any new crop worth trying?. . and so on.

Choosing Seeds

While you are working on the plan, you should also be thinking about seeds and exactly what crops you want to grow. There are no definite rules here; the final choice is yours, and will depend on the size of your plot, the type of soil, where you live and what you like to eat. But it makes sense to try to balance economy and the profitable use of your ground with the culinary interest and value of your crops. The traditional and most obvious answer is to grow large quantities of a small number of crops that provide good yields—potatoes, broad beans, brassicas, and so on. This is quite reasonable if you have an allotment or large piece of ground; you can work out a rotation and grow as many crops as you wish. But if you have only a little plot, you may want to devote it to just potatoes, or salad vegetables, or even to a few very unusual items; you may need to improvise—putting marrows in tubs, growing runner beans against a wall. So think ahead when you are planning.

I have talked about seeds and seed catalogues and have given a suggested list of varieties in the Introduction (see pp. 19-20). Study this, don't treat it as the only possible selection. Finally, when you have decided what seeds you want, order them as early as possible. It is also advisable to give the seed merchant a second choice in case he has run out of the variety that you particularly want.

Seed Potatoes

It is important to order seed potatoes early, so that they can be put into trays to sprout, and so be planted in good time. Potatoes can really be divided into three groups:

earlies—ready in July
second earlies—ready in August
maincrop—ready from late September onwards.

For most practical purposes it is best to think simply of earlies and maincrop.

First you must decide which you want to grow, and then the specific variety. If you have plenty of ground you can grow earlies and maincrop; on a small plot you can either grow earlies for their special flavour, or maincrop for economy and a good supply of potatoes that can be stored through the winter. If you have grown potatoes before and have had good crops from a particular variety, then it is worth continuing with it. If not, ask a local friend or neighbour for suggestions; this will give you a guide as to which varieties do best in your soil and locality.

Seed potatoes like all seeds are not cheap, so it is important to calculate fairly accurately how many you are going to need. A simple guide is that a 30ft. row can be planted with 4lbs of earlies or 3lbs of maincrop. When you order, tell the seed merchant that you will accept another variety; give him a choice. This will save a lot of time.

Aim to have your first new potatoes ready in July, and sufficient in the ground to last until September when the first maincrop will be ready. These in turn should last through the winter and well into the spring if properly stored.

Crops in the Soil

This month you should try to use up most of the crops still left in the soil. By 'storing' some vegetables like this you will not only have saved space in the shed and kitchen, but also improved the flavour of the crops themselves.

Jerusalem artichokes

These should be left in the ground as long as possible, but it is worth lifting them all this month, otherwise they may become unmanageable. Also it will give you a chance to clear and dig the ground properly. When you lift the tubers put aside a few choice ones for replanting once you have dug the patch; good egg-sized tubers are best. The others can be stored in the shed or cellar in boxes covered lightly with some loose soil.

Jerusalem artichokes can be planted in any neglected corner of the garden; they grow up to 8ft high, form excellent windbreaks, and give valuable shade to salad vegetables in summer. Dig the

Jerusalem artichokes take up space, but are easy to grow and make a tasty winter dish.

patch deeply, putting in leaf mould or vegetable refuse, and be ready to plant the tubers next month.

Every garden should have artichokes. They are excellent food, even though people complain that they are knobbly and impossible to peel. Eat them if you are short of potatoes, pickle them with lemon peel, make soups and fill out stews and casseroles with them.

Parsnips

These will have been ready for use in November, and can be left in the ground until required. But when you notice new green growth beginning, they must all be lifted and stored.

Frost improves their flavour, but if the ground is frozen hard, it is difficult to dig the roots without splitting them. So in very cold weather put some straw over the parsnips to protect them. If the weather stays very wet, it is best to lift all the roots and store them straight away. Cut off the top growth and let the roots dry out for a day or so—under cover if necessary. Then either pack them in boxes of sand like carrots, or stack them neatly in a dry shed and cover with sacking.

Leeks

Continue to use up leeks. They keep well in the ground. But they do not store so well as some other vegetables. Dig them only when you need them.

Celery

The plants will keep in the soil through the winter, provided that they have been well earthed-up. In rough weather cover the exposed tops with straw for protection. Unless the weather is very cold or wet, simply lift plants when you need them. It's a good idea to lift several plants if there are signs of a hard frost, as it is difficult to dig them up when the ground is frozen.

You must be careful when lifting celery to avoid breaking the sticks. Use

Holding the tops with your free hand, lift celery carefully to avoid damaging the edible sticks.

a spade, and scrape away all the soil from one side of the plant. This will loosen the plant and help you to see where the roots begin. Drive the spade downwards, at a slant, and lever the whole plant out of the soil.

The sticks are the main part of the celery, but don't throw away the leaves; they make a useful flavouring— important at a time of year when herbs may be hard to come by.

Fresh pickings

You should have plenty of fresh greens to pick this month: brussels sprouts, winter cabbages (Savoy, January King, Drumhead, etc), cauliflowers and also late spinach.

Pick sprouts as you need them, working from the base of the stalk upwards. Don't forget the brussels tops—these are marvellous young greens that can be picked when the sprouts have been cleared.

Cut cabbages when you need them. Put the outer leaves and decaying matter on to your new compost heap, but don't throw the stumps and roots on to the heap when you dig them up. They must be smashed and either burned or put to rot with other refuse. (This applies to brussels sprouts as well.)

If you want to get an extra crop from your cabbages, you can stimulate fresh growth by making a couple of cuts across the top of the stump after you have taken the head. Don't take off the outer leaves in this case, and quite soon new tufts of greens will begin to form on the stump. Exactly the same trick was used by gardeners in the middle ages, and apparently they could get as many as four crops from a single cabbage plant.

Cauliflowers, kale and broccoli suffer badly from frost at this time of year, and may look in a sorry state. Protect the heads by folding or tying the outer leaves over them.

Stores

You should still have a fair amount of food stored and ready for use: potatoes, carrots, swedes, turnips, onions, beetroot, marrows and possibly a few heavy white cabbages. Keep a check on these stores throughout the winter and watch for any signs of decay, or thieving by rats and mice. It is essential to get rid of any vegetables that are soft or mouldy before they ruin the rest of your store.

Shallots that you are keeping for planting out next month should also be watched.

FEBRUARY

"Here learne to knowe
what seeds to sowe."

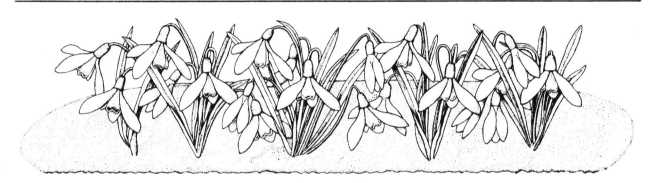

This month often has the worst weather of the year. It tends to be damp, wet and depressing. It is the lowest ebb of winter. Occasionally the sun appears, and you are deceived into thinking that spring has arrived early. Hopes rise, only to be dashed again as the wind sets in, the rain pours and it freezes.

In the early months of the year, work in the garden is really dictated by the weather. The soil may be so cold that it is pointless even considering any seed sowing, or the land may be so wet that it is impossible even to get on it, as it sticks to your boots. And digging may be out of the question if frost has reduced the soil to iron. But, with luck, there should be several days when you can get out and do some useful work.

The most important event will be the first sowing of hardy crops like shallots, broad beans and spinach. Shallots are always the very first crop I plant outside each year, so they take on a special significance. Once they are in—even if the weather is dreary—I know that the growing year has begun, the worst is almost over, and before too long I shall be hoeing.

Summary
1) Seeds and seed potatoes.
2) First planting and sowing: shallots, Jerusalem artichokes, broad beans, spinach.
3) Tending to early crops: spring cabbage, broccoli.
4) General work: using winter crops, making a hot-bed, forcing rhubarb.

Seeds and seed potatoes

If you ordered your seeds early, they should have arrived by now. Check that you have received what you ordered and put the packets away in a safe, dry place at room temperature until they are required.

You must deal with seed potatoes straight away. Get hold of some shallow wooden boxes—old seed trays are ideal—and carefully sort out the potatoes. Treat them gently from now until they are in the soil. If you look at the potatoes you will see several sunken buds or eyes; these produce the shoots and the best are situated at the broad or 'rose' end of each tuber.

Pack the potatoes into boxes with their rose ends upwards, in a single layer. To form short, sturdy green shoots they must be exposed to the light and must be put in a dry place; warmth isn't essential, but they should be stored where there is no danger of exposure to extreme cold or frost. Keep an eye on the potatoes as they begin to sprout, throw out any that look suspect and begin to limit the number of shoots on each tuber. This is important. If you plant a potato covered with shoots, it will be a weak plant, with a lot of foliage but a poor yield. Simply rub off

Seed potatoes arranged in seed boxes. The growing shoots should be limited to two good ones at the rose end.

unwanted weak shoots as they develop and aim to finish up with two good shoots at the rose end of each tuber. (If the potato is very large, leave more shoots, so that it can be split in half before planting.)

If you notice that the shoots are becoming long and spindly it means that the trays are not in the right place; they need more light.

First planting and sowing

Shallots
Traditionally shallots were planted on the shortest day, and lifted on the longest, but with the shifts in seasonal conditions it is much wiser to plant them in February and lift in July.

For the first year you will need to buy the bulbs, but after that you can save a few from your own crop, store them through the winter, and use them as next year's 'seed'. Shallots don't need much space, and each bulb produces on average 8-10 new shallots. Plant the bulbs in a piece of well-dug soil in full sun, which was manured last autumn. Make sure the soil is firm; if necessary tread it until there are no signs of looseness. Scatter a few handfuls of wood ash over the soil and rake this in lightly.

Planting is quite simple. You can either make a flat-bottomed drill about 2in deep with a draw hoe, set the bulbs 9in apart and bury them so that they are half-covered; or you can make individual holes and set the shallots into place—again so that they are half-buried. Be careful not to damage the base or root end of the shallots while planting them. If you want more than one row, space them 1ft apart.

You will need to look at the shallots every day for about a week as they are often disturbed by birds, cats and even strong winds. This only happens before the shallots have had time to anchor

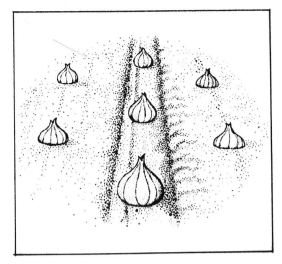

Shallots should not be pressed in, but planted firmly, 9in apart, and half-covered with soil.

themselves with roots, but can be a real nuisance. There is not much you can do about this, except to ensure that the shallots are properly planted rather than pushed into the soil, and to keep your eyes open.

Jerusalem artichokes

Good tubers saved from last month can now be planted in the ground prepared for them. If the tubers are very large, they can be divided into two or even three smaller pieces, making sure that each portion has an 'eye'. One row is usually enough. Put a line down, and take out a drill 4-6in deep with a spade; plant the tubers 1ft apart and cover with 4in of soil. If you want more than one row, there must be 3ft between them.

In very heavy soil it may be easier to dig individual holes for each tuber, planting them 4in deep and 1ft apart as above. Unlike potatoes, Jerusalem artichokes do not need earthing up.

Broad beans

If the weather is good and you can get on the land without mud caking to your boots, the first sowings of broad beans can be made in the second half of the month. They should then be ready for picking at the end of June or beginning of July. Choose an exposed piece of ground that has been well dug and manured. If possible set the rows running north to south; take out a drill 9in wide and 6in deep with a spade and sow the beans in this, spacing the seeds 4in apart in a staggered double row. Cover with 3in of soil. You can alternatively use a line and dibber and plant the seeds individually 3in deep, and 4in apart as before. The advantage of the first method is that during dry weather all available water can collect in the trench. This is a general rule for many seeds, particularly if the soil is light. It also helps if you water the drill or trench before sowing the seeds in dry weather.

Sow a few extra seeds at the end of each drill; these can be used to fill any

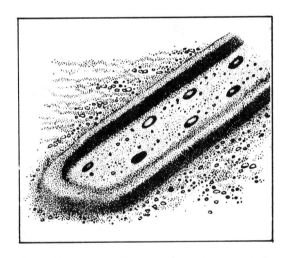

Broad beans can be sown in a staggered double row to give the plants extra self-support.

gaps in the rows where seeds do not germinate.

A reminder about broad beans sown in the autumn: in hard weather the young plants should be covered with straw. Remove this when you think the danger of frost damage is past. These beans should be producing pods about two weeks earlier than the first spring sowings.

February

Spinach

At the end of the month sow the first round-seeded (summer) spinach. Be sure to distinguish between this plant and winter spinach, which has prickly seeds. Summer spinach needs a rich, moist soil and the seeds should be sown where there is plenty of shade. It is not worth sowing in light soil unless this has been well-manured or enriched with leaf mould; the plants simply bolt after the slightest drought. An ideal spot is between rows of broad beans. This 'intercropping' is a space saver; the soil is rich and the beans will provide plenty of shade for the spinach. It helps germination if you soak the seeds in very lukewarm water for 24 hours before sowing. Make drills 1ft apart and put groups of three seeds at 8in intervals along each drill and cover with 1in of soil. This is better than sowing in a continuous row as it saves seeds and makes thinning much easier: each group is simply reduced to one plant.

Tending to early crops

As well as broad beans there are other crops, planted last autumn, which should have survived the cold weather.

Spring cabbage

If the weather has been bad, these may have suffered; they are particularly vulnerable to frost and severe cold. Take out any plants that have died, and replace them with extra plants from other rows. As the weather gets warmer a few weeds may begin to appear. Keep these down with a hoe.

Broccoli

The various types of sprouting broccoli which can be picked up to the end of April may need examining occasionally. If the plants were heeled over to protect them during bad weather, they should now be firmed in the soil and all dead leaves removed.

General work

Using winter crops

Continue to lift winter crops: leeks, celery and parsnips. Gather brussels sprouts and cut savoy cabbages. Use up other root crops like carrots, swedes and turnips from your stores.

Making a hot-bed

If you can get hold of stable manure it is worth making a simple outdoor hot-bed. Build a heap of well-rotted manure and leaf mould at least 2ft deep, and cover this with a 6in layer of good soil, well broken up and free from weeds or rubbish. This bed can be used for sowing radishes, turnips, carrots and so on. For early sowings, the soil can be covered with a glass frame or cloche.

Forcing rhubarb

Established crowns can be forced slowly outdoors to provide early spring crops. Put old buckets or barrels over the crowns with plenty of well-rotted, warm manure or fermenting leaves. You should be pulling sticks of rhubarb by April.

If you want to build a new rhubarb bed then February is the best month to begin. The ground must be well-dug and not too shaded. Dig to a depth of 2ft if possible and add as much manure or rotted greenstuff as possible at the bottom of the bed.

The best way to begin a rhubarb bed is to plant root clumps. These should be put in so that the tops are covered with at least 2in of soil; a little bone meal added to the top soil will help growth. The root clumps should have one or two crowns or buds and should be set 3ft apart. Roots must have one whole season in the ground before any sticks are pulled.

MARCH

"To weeding away
as soon as ye may."

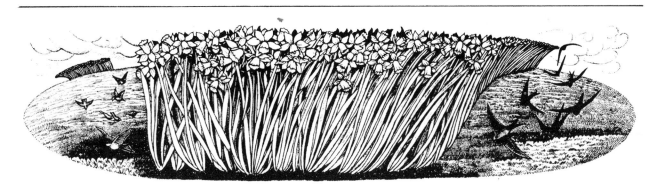

The garden really begins to come to life in March. There is usually a good deal of sunshine and it is getting warmer. So it is time to sow plenty of seeds. A few sowings were made last month, but now you can get to work with more broad beans, spinach, carrots, lettuce, potatoes and onions; some of these can go into the newly made seed-bed or on to the outdoor hot-bed.

March sees the last of the winter crops like sprouts and celery, and the first spring cabbages, sprouting broccoli and cauliflowers. Crops that have been dormant right through the winter will now begin to show new green shoots, responding to the light and warmth.

Because the weather is getting much warmer, weeds will also begin to germinate. So it is time to start the long, almost perpetual job of hoeing. Between now and September the hoe will be your best tool for defeating weeds. I like hoeing. It is something that can be done briskly on a cold morning, or at a snail's pace on a hot summer day. The perfect excuse for standing out in the sun.

Summary
1) Final preparation of the land: clearing and breaking down the soil, making a seed-bed, trenches for runner beans and celery, the asparagus bed, hoeing.
2) Sowings: potatoes, parsnips, carrots, turnips, lettuce, onions, garlic, seed-bed sowings.

3) Herbs and the herb garden.
4) Pickings: spring cabbage, kale, winter crops.

Final preparation of the land

Clearing and breaking down soil
You must try to have all your winter crops cleared from the land by the beginning of the month. If you find that you still have a great many celery or leek plants, lift them and heel them in a spare corner of the garden. This will save them, stop them running to seed and it will leave the land free for new crops. Make sure that celery is well covered with earth to keep it crisp and white.

Once the soil is dry enough you can begin to go through it with a fork, breaking up the large clods left from winter digging. If the frost has done its work, this should be an easy task. But a warning: if the soil is wet, and particularly if it is heavy as well, don't attempt this work because it can do a great deal of harm to the land. Test the soil with your boots. If it cakes and feels sticky, it is too wet.

Making a seed-bed
Choose a suitable corner of your garden for use as a seed-bed. It doesn't need to be very big as its main job will be to act as a germinating ground for seeds of leeks, brassicas, etc., which are later transplanted on to the main plot. Break down the soil with a fork until you have a fine tilth; and then work through it with a rake, clearing any stones and debris to give a fine, even surface ready for sowing. Don't do this work until the soil is dry.

Trenches for runner beans and celery
Decide where you are going to grow celery and runner beans and dig the trenches for these crops. For runners, organize the trench so that it runs north-south and take out the soil to a depth of 1ft, or deeper if you are going to add more manure. Throw the soil up alongside the trench and allow it to weather for several weeks.

A similar trench should be made for celery, about 18in wide and about 1ft deep; the bottom of the trench is broken

A small, well-prepared seed-bed is essential in the vegetable garden. It is the germinating ground for many seeds such as leeks and the brassicas. A fine, moist tilth should be continuously maintained.

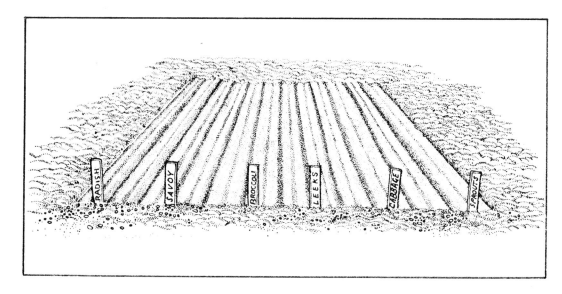

up, and manure and bonemeal can be forked into the soil. When you dig the trench heap the soil alongside it as for runner bean trench. This need not be wasted; in fact, it is a good spot for planting short rows of lettuce or spinach.

The asparagus bed

This is a luxury, and if you have a well established bed you are lucky. But think before you decide to put in a new one. The crop has a short season, the bed will take up a fair amount of space and it is a permanent site. But, in this country at least, asparagus is fast becoming an uneconomical crop for large growers. This is because of the labour involved in cutting the sticks, asparagus has a short season, and the ground cannot be used for anything else once that season is over. So my final advice is make an asparagus bed if you can possibly find the space. Save yourself money, enjoy the crop fresh from your garden and help to make sure that it doesn't disappear altogether from this country.

Asparagus, like rhubarb, is a 'permanent' crop and a hungry one too. So the ground must be deeply dug and have as much bonemeal and manure added as possible; the ground itself also needs to be well-drained. The actual size of the bed will depend on what space you can spare, but a useful guide is to make a plot 4½ft wide which will accommodate two rows, 18in apart. Mark out the rows with a garden line and take out a trench 5in deep with a spade. Do this as early as possible.

Now for the plants themselves. Asparagus needs to be 3 years old before you can start cutting, so the best policy is to buy root clumps 1 or 2 years old. Treat them very gently and lay them in the trenches, spreading the roots in all directions; there should be 15in between the tips of each clump. Cover with soil, making sure you don't damage the delicate crowns or growing points.

Give the bed a good watering as soon as you have planted the asparagus.

Finally you can dig out a path around the bed and pile the soil on to the bed so that it is distinct and separate from the rest of the plot.

Established asparagus beds may also need some attention. Tidy them up generally, and throw back any soil that has been washed on to the 'path'.

Hoeing

As the weather becomes warmer, weeds will begin to show. These must be kept down with a dutch hoe. Go through all the growing crops and clear ground as often as possible. The regular movement of the soil not only keeps down weeds, but helps to retain moisture by blocking air holes and cracks—and this is important during the growing season.

Sowings

Make second sowings of broad beans and round-seeded spinach during March, and also a number of first sowings.

Potatoes

There is no point in trying to plant potatoes too early or the tender foliage will appear while there is still a danger of frost. The ground must be warm enough otherwise they will simply lie dormant; it is also not worth planting the tubers until they have sprouted properly. But, by the second half of the month, if the weather is warm, the first earlies can be planted.

Look at the tubers and pick out those that are healthy, with a couple of sturdy shoots at the rose end; larger tubers can be cut in half before planting, so that each half has two shoots.

Mark out the rows with a line—north to south if possible, so that they get full benefit from the sun. Take out trenches

4-6in deep with a spade or hoe; the lighter the soil the deeper you should plant. Treat the tubers with care; don't bundle them into a bag or basket when you take them out to the garden, but keep them in their trays. These earlies should be planted 1ft apart in rows which are set 2ft apart. Put the tubers into the trench, sprouts upwards, and pack some soil around them with your hands before filling in the trench. Then use a hoe or the back of a rake to cover the tubers completely; do this gently so that you do not damage the shoots. At this stage there is no need to ridge the rows; this can be done later when the plants are showing. Mark the rows at each end with sticks.

Parsnips

If possible try to sow parsnips where beans, peas or celery did well last year. The deeply-dug, well-manured soil suits them well. The seeds should be sown as early as possible because they take a long time to germinate and tend to grow quite slowly in their early stages. But don't try to sow them until you have forked and raked the soil to a fine tilth; a sprinkling of wood ash mixed in with the top soil will help the crop. Try to get out as many stones as you can, as these may cause the roots to fork.

Take out 1in drills, 15in apart with a hoe, and sow the seeds, not in a continuous row, but in groups of 4 or 5 seeds at 12in intervals. When the seedlings are about 2in high, they can be thinned out to single plants. Be careful if you sow the seeds on a windy day, as many of them may blow away if you scatter them carelessly into the drill.

People who grow parsnips more for show than for food will go to great lengths to produce very long roots. They use a method of boring individual holes with a crowbar, similar to that described for sowing carrots in very heavy soil (see p. 45). But these unnatural looking specimens are often almost inedible because they have such a long fibrous core.

Carrots

The first sowings of carrots can be made any time in March under normal conditions. The thinnings will be ready for pulling as new carrots in June. Carrots do best in light sandy soil provided it is rich enough. Remember that 'light' soil is not the same as 'thin' soil, which is poor, and needs a lot of leaf-mould and wood ash to make it suitable for carrots. Very heavy clay soils generally do not produce good crops of carrots, even if the ground has been well prepared. Above all, don't sow carrots, or other root crops, in freshly manured ground.

Mark out the rows with a line, and then take out drills ½in deep and allow about 9in between each row. You can either sow the seeds like parsnips in groups, or thinly in a continuous row. This is better because you can pull plenty of thinnings as new carrots—either eaten raw in salads or cooked without scraping as a summer vegetable.

Turnips

Turnips like a rich soil, and these early sowings are best put in a warm sheltered spot. Take out drills ½in deep and 9in apart and sow thinly in a continuous row like carrots. It will help germination if the seeds are soaked in water the day before sowing. The seedlings will need thinning so that they are finally 6in apart. The thinnings, however, are useful as small summer roots. Make more sowings in April and May. The first turnips should be ready for use about 8 weeks after sowing. (For winter crops you will need to sow again in August and September.)

Lettuce

Aim to have a succession of lettuces right through the summer, and even through the winter if you wish. There are many varieties to choose from these days, and also specific varieties for spring and autumn sowing. Don't make the mistake of sowing the wrong variety, and then wonder why it does not grow. In general, lettuces like rich moist ground and a quick growing season to produce good hearts. They also like a sunny, but sheltered, position so they are ideally planted between rows of beans or peas. If your soil tends to be rather thin and dry then, as a rule, you are likely to have more success with cabbage varieties rather than cos, for they do not bolt so readily under dry conditions.

Once you have prepared a site so that the soil is well broken up and reduced to a fine tilth, make drills ½in deep and sow just a few seeds in the drill. Don't empty a whole packet into the drill—this is simply a waste—but sow a few seeds in succession, say every 10 days, so that you have a row of lettuces at different stages. For normal requirements aim to have about 6 lettuces ready for use at any time, several almost ready, some needing thinning and so on up the row. The soil must never be allowed to dry out; keep it well watered. For the earliest sowings it is a good idea to cover the rows with cloches; this helps germination and protects the seedlings.

Onions

There is always a great deal of argument about the merits of onion seeds and onion sets—small immature bulbs which are planted like shallots. I have tried both and have always had more success with sets. If the ground has been well-prepared they are certainly less trouble to grow: they don't need thinning or transplanting, they are less vulnerable to onion fly, and in my experience they produce better quality onions. If you are growing onions for the first time it is a good idea to try both methods to see which is most suited to your garden.

Onions are one of the few crops which can be grown in the same spot year after year, provided that the ground has been properly prepared during the winter. The only exception to this is if the onions become infested with eelworm or onion fly. In this case you should not use the ground for onions or other bulbs for three years.

Onion sets: March is the best month for planting sets. The ground should have been deeply dug and enriched in the late autumn (see p. 88) and, more important, it should be very firm. This can be done by treading or even rolling when the ground is dry, just before you want to plant. Mark out drills and plant the onions like shallots (see pp. 34-35); space them 6in apart and firm them in the soil so that they are half-covered. Like shallots they can be disturbed by birds and the wind before the roots have formed properly. If this happens simply firm them back in position.

Onion seeds: These can also be sown in early March. Make drills ¾in deep and 1ft apart and either sprinkle the seeds lightly in a continuous row, or put a few seeds at 4-6in intervals. The first method has the advantage that the onion thinnings can be used in salads, leaving the remaining bulbs 6in apart to develop as the maincrop. Make sure that the seeds are well covered and the surface firmed.

Onions sown in the autumn, and left through the winter, can be thinned during March.

Garlic

Garlic can be planted like shallots or onion sets. It does best in light, rich soil, and quantities of wood ash or old soot will help the crop if forked into the soil before planting. The bulbs of garlic are separated into 'cloves' and these are planted 9in apart in drills and buried 2in deep. The crop needs little attention except hoeing and very occasional watering if the weather is dry.

March

Once your seed-bed is ready and the weather is warm enough, there are several crops that need to be sown.

Cabbage

These spring-sown cabbages will be ready for cutting in the autumn. Make drills ½in deep in the seed-bed and sow the seed thinly. Never waste seeds. If the weather is dry it may be worth watering the drills before sowing, and you must water the seedlings regularly during the early stages. Later they need to be thinned, and finally transplanted when they are 3-4in high.

Brussels sprouts

These need to be started as early as possible as they have a long growing season. Treat them like cabbages.

Broccoli

Winter heading broccoli should also be sown now, and can be treated in the same way as cabbage.

Leeks

These also need a long growing season, and can be sown thinly in ½in drills this month. If the weather allows, it may be worth making two smaller sowings—one early in the month, the other 2-3 weeks later. This will give you a longer supply of leeks from October onwards.

Herbs and the herb garden

Herbs are an important part of the food garden. There is a vast number of species to choose from, you can buy them as seeds or as young plants and you can take cuttings as well. Try and grow as many as you can: not only the common ones like parsley, thyme, sage and one variety of mint, but also marjoram, fennel, basil, tarragon, etc. Then there are the rarities: plants with

Always make use of as many herbs, wild plants and 'weeds' as you can.

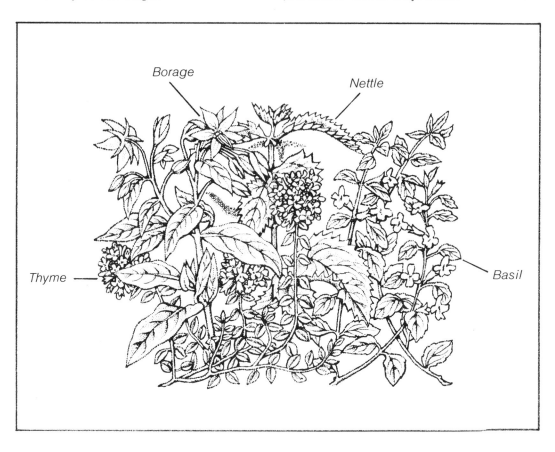

Borage

Nettle

Thyme

Basil

ancient names like hyssop, rocket, southernwood, purslane, costmary, and yet others like horseradish and dandelion which today are thought of as mere weeds. Instead of pulling these up wherever you find them, cultivate and encourage a few—in other words *use* them. There are other plants like this, for instance alexanders and hedge garlic which are much more valuable in the kitchen than on the rubbish heap.

So the idea of herbs in the garden isn't confined to that little patch outside the kitchen door.

Generally the herb garden needs to be in a sunny position, and the soil needs to be rich, well-dug but not too heavy. It is not possible here to give detailed accounts of all herbs and how each one is cultivated, and most of them do need special treatment of one kind or another. But I should like to encourage people to think about herbs, and to explore the possibilities. There are a great many books on the subject, but one useful book—particularly for beginners—is *The Penguin Book of Herbs and Spices* by Rosemary Hemphill. This will give you plenty of basic information about herb growing, and from there you can move on to more detailed accounts of less well-known herbs.

Spring crops

Spring cabbage

These should be almost ready for cutting. If they seem rather close together, take out the weakest first, and use them as spring greens. The others can be left to heart up as cabbages proper.

Kale

The different types of kale are invaluable winter foods as they are available when other crops can be scarce. Pick off a few leaves or shoots at a time from various plants. When the stems have been stripped clean, dig them up and either burn the stumps for wood ash or smash them up and put them to rot.

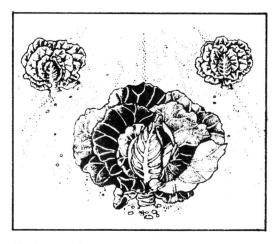

Spring cabbages should be cut as soon as the hearts feel firm. Later they can become tough and bitter.

Last of the winter crops

There may still be a few sprouts and brussels tops worth picking, leeks which may be getting rather fibrous, but are still good for soup, some spinach and the last savoys, and there may still be some root crops in your shed or storehouse. Use these up quickly now, for with the warmer weather they will not last much longer.

APRIL

"Make readie a plot
for seeds for the pot."

The days are beginning to get longer, but April can be a deceptive month. The weather may turn in the space of an hour from hopeful spring sunshine to cold, vicious winds and pouring rain. You should be ready to do a great deal of work if the weather is good: seeds planted for salads later in the year, more deep rows of potatoes. Bad weather brings both work and the growth of crops to a standstill: broad beans and the first shoots of early potatoes are at their most vulnerable if the temperature drops and the frost strikes at them.

April is really the time for sowing and planting all the early summer crops—roots, salad vegetables, legumes—but there are still good things to eat from the garden. There are spring cabbages at their best, the very last leeks, young spring rhubarb, spinach. And by the end of the month you will see the pink-tipped spears of asparagus beginning to emerge. This is a hopeful sign. But the sticks are not ready for cutting, so instead you must make do with the last shoots of purple sprouting broccoli cooked and eaten with melted butter. Before long these plants will be in flower and will need to be dug out to make room for beans and other late summer crops.

Summary
1) General work: frost protection, weeding.
2) Sowing: beetroot, carrots, kohl-rabi, celeriac, radishes, salsify, calabrese, cauliflowers, peas, successional sowings.
3) Planting: potatoes, globe artichokes.

4) *Fresh crops: sprouting broccoli, spring greens, turnip tops, leeks, rhubarb.*

General work

If you have kept ahead with work in the garden during February and March, most of the heavy work will be finished by now. But there are still a number of smaller jobs which need to be dealt with.

Frost is one danger that you must be aware of. Young shoots of broad beans and early potatoes are very vulnerable to attack, and should be earthed up or protected with a layer of straw.

Weeds will be starting to appear, and must be kept down with a hoe. This is particularly important with crops like asparagus which are developing quickly—the first spears will emerge this month. The remnants of the dried stems from last year's crop will tell you where the crowns are located, but you should be very careful not to damage the new shoots.

Sowing

Beetroot
Don't sow beetroot in freshly manured ground. Either sow them in a patch that has recently been cleared of leeks or celery, or prepare some new ground and add a quantity of wood ash when you are digging (see p. 23).

The seeds are slow to germinate, particularly if the soil is 'cold', so it is worth waiting until the end of the month before you sow. Take out drills 1in deep and 1ft apart with a hoe, and sow the seeds quite thickly in a continuous row rather than at intervals, as the seeds tend to have a higher failure rate than most others. You can thin the crop and use the baby beets in June and July for salads, and for pickling whole. This will leave the plants 6in apart to develop until the autumn. It is not worth transplanting beetroot.

During the growing season, the plants can be given more wood ash which is hoed and watered along the rows.

Carrots
Sow long-rooted carrots which are best grown in deep, but light soil. The seeds are sown in $\frac{1}{2}$in drills like early varieties.

Carrots can be grown in heavy soil, but will need special treatment. Bore individual holes—say 18in deep and 3in across—with a crowbar, and fill these with a light mixed soil. Sprinkle a few seeds on top of each hole and cover with a thin layer of soil. When the seeds germinate they can be thinned out so that only one remains for each bore-hole.

Kohl-rabi
This is an odd-looking vegetable, but it is delicious to eat. In fact it tastes exactly like a cross between turnip and cabbage. It is an easy crop to grow, and a hardy one as well; it thrives even in dry light soil, it is hardly affected by drought or frost, and is a useful alternative to summer turnips. Of course, if you can sow it in rich, well-dug soil so much the better. Take out drills $\frac{3}{4}$in deep and 18in apart, and sow the seeds thinly. As they develop, they can be thinned out, finally leaving the plants 10in apart. As the base of the stems begin to swell, scrape the soil away from them, so that growth is not hindered.

Kohl-rabi from these early sowings will be ready for pulling in July, and by sowing a short row every three weeks, you will have a good supply through the summer. If you want kohl-rabi in the autumn or winter, you can make late sowings at the end of July.

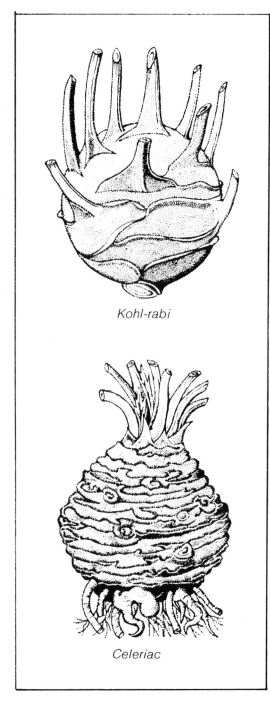

Kohl-rabi

Celeriac

Two unusual vegetables. Kohl-rabi is ready to eat in the summer and celeriac in the autumn.

Celeriac

Another curious vegetable—this time a cross between turnip and celery. Again the swollen base is the edible part. You can start this crop by sowing seeds in the seed-bed in drills ¼in deep. Later the plants will need thinning to 3in apart, and in June they can be transplanted to the main plot in a patch of rich, well-dug soil with plenty of sun. The crop should be ready for eating from October onwards.

Radishes

It is not really worth sowing radishes until this month unless you are particularly addicted to them. They grow quickly, in 6-8 weeks and should be sown regularly from April onwards. They are best intercropped between rows of slow-growing crops like beans.

Don't sow too much seed as this is simply wasteful. A short row sown very thinly every 2-3 weeks will provide you with as many radishes as you can eat. For summer salads you can grow either spherical or long varieties. They need a quick growing season, they should be thinned early, leaving the radishes 3in apart, and they should be pulled as soon as they have reached a reasonable size. Don't leave them in the ground until they are like golf-balls as they will be tough, spongy and unpleasant. But any radishes from these early sowings which are not pulled can be left in the ground, allowed to flower and the seed-pods harvested and pickled for winter salads.

(There are several varieties of winter radish that are worth growing, and these should be sown in the autumn.)

Salsify

Nicknamed the vegetable oyster, because of its taste, salsify is an easy and interesting crop to grow. It needs a sunny position and light soil so that its long roots—the edible part—can penetrate and grow properly.

Make 1in drills and sow the seeds at intervals along the row; put 2 or 3 seeds every 9in and thin them down to single seedlings when they are a couple of inches high.

Salsify, sown in April, will be ready in October and, if the soil is light and dry, can be left in the ground until required.

Scorzonera can be grown like salsify. It is a similar vegetable, except that its roots are black skinned.

Calabrese

This variety of broccoli—sometimes called Italian green sprouting broccoli—can be sown in the seed-bed during April. Take out drills ½in deep and sow a thin continuous row. After the plants have been thinned, they can be transplanted when 3-4in high to the main plot, and the large greenish heads will be ready to cut in August or September. After this the plants continue to produce a number of smaller sprouts.

Cauliflower

The seed can be sown in the sed-bed in the same way as calabrese. They will produce curds ready for eating in the early autumn.

Peas

It is possible to sow peas in February or early March, but unless the weather is unusually good, it is best to wait until late March or the beginning of April before you start. It does no good to sow the seeds in wet, cold soil, as they will remain dormant, and might even decay.

If you are going to grow peas, it is essential to make a number of fairly large sowings. One row will give you a few meals, but it takes up a lot of space, and is not worth the trouble if you want to make the best use of your land. So set aside an area for the crop, make several sowings, and with proper cultivation you should have pounds of peas right through the summer.

Peas thrive on rich, deeply dug soil that has been well manured, preferably the previous autumn. Mark out rows running north to south if possible and then either take out single drills with the edge of a hoe, or make a flat-bottomed drill, 6-8in wide, which can take 2 or 3 rows of peas. In both cases make the drills 3in deep. Sow the seeds at 2in intervals along the rows and space the rows according to the height of the plants; e.g. varieties which grow to a height of 1½ft should be sown in rows 1½ft apart and so on. If the soil is dry when you intend to sow, it is a good idea to soak the drills an hour before sowing.

In late March and early April, sow early varieties, which grow to 1½-2ft; then from May onwards sow maincrop (3-5ft). Sow a new row as soon as seedlings from the previous sowing have begun to show.

Once peas are in the soil they are vulnerable to attack, particularly from mice and birds, so they must be protected. You can hang tin cans or other noisy containers on a line to scare birds, and it is sensible to cover the rows immediately with wire-netting arches or cloches—remembering to block off the open ends of the rows. When the seedlings are established you will need to support them with sticks. These should be slightly taller than the final height of the plants and should be pushed in firmly, so that they lean

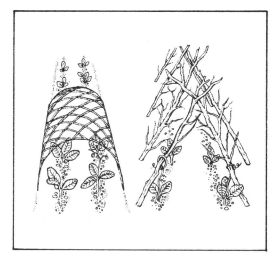

Protect young peas with wire-netting covers and later support the plants with twiggy sticks pushed firmly into the ground on each side of the row.

inwards slightly. Even the dwarf varieties are best supported. Apart from protection, the sticks allow the plants to grow up rather than straggling on the ground. This makes picking much easier and lessens the chance of damage to the plants and crop.

Put a mulch of old lawn mowings round the rows to prevent the ground from losing valuable moisture in hot weather, and water the plants, particularly after the pods have formed.

Successional sowings
In April you should also make further sowings of turnips, lettuce and cabbages (including red cabbage) for the autumn. Also broad beans, if the weather has delayed early sowings.

Begin to earth up potatoes with a draw hoe once the foliage has started to show.

Planting

Potatoes
At the end of the month you can begin to plant maincrop potatoes. The actual planting is the same as for earlies, except that the maincrop tubers are spaced 15in apart in the rows. My own favourite is undoubtedly the firm, pink-skinned Desiree which produces heavy crops and is also blight resistant. I have even tried these as 'earlies': when they are small they taste like West Indian sweet potatoes.

People occasionally talk about potatoes as if they had almost magical properties for 'clearing the ground'. Of course, this has nothing to do with the potatoes themselves. Any beneficial effect on the land comes from the work you do—the planting, earthing up and finally the lifting of the potatoes. There can be severe frosts during April, so you must protect the shoots of early potatoes by earthing up the soil around the plants. As they develop continue earthing up until you have a wide-based ridge along each row. The main purpose of earthing up is to keep the tubers well covered with soil and to prevent them from appearing on the surface, where they would rapidly turn green.

Globe artichokes
If you want to grow these, the easiest plan is to buy young plants, or take suckers (rooted offsets) from established plants. This is much more effective than trying to grow them from seed.

The soil needs to be rich, well-drained and in an open sunny position. Plant the suckers in rows 2½ft apart with 2ft between each plant. Make sure that they are firm. If you are taking suckers from established plants, remove them carefully and make sure that each sucker has roots, then plant as above.

The globes—or unopened flower heads—are ready for cutting in July. The crop needs plenty of water in dry weather, and extra leaf mould or rotted greenstuff dug in during the summer will help growth. The plants are good for about 4 years; after this they need to be dug up and replaced.

Fresh Crops

Sprouting broccoli
This is a good time for purple sprouting broccoli. Pick the delicate shoots regularly before they become spindly; cook them quickly and serve them steeped in melted butter. They can be eaten with the fingers like asparagus. As the plants are used up they can be cleared and the land prepared for other crops.

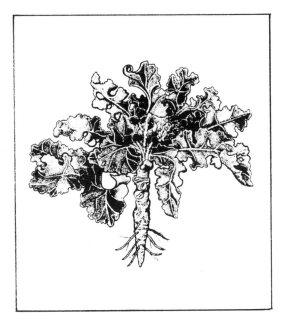

Purple sprouting broccoli shoots should be picked before they start to run to flower.

Spring greens, cabbage and kale
All these should be ready for early pickings. The spring cabbage should have started to heart up, but may need a little more time, so don't pick too soon.

Turnip tops
The tops from turnips are a useful spring vegetable, particularly if there are not many other greens in the garden. Sort out the best leaves and throw any very old or decaying ones onto the compost heap. Wash the others well, and cook in a little water like spinach.

Leeks
These may be getting rather tough and fibrous, but are still worth using, particularly in soups and stews where they can be cooked for a long time, very slowly.

Rhubarb
The first sticks of spring rhubarb should be ready for pulling. Once they have turned pinkish-red and the leaves have flattened towards the ground you can begin to take them. Always pull by grasping the sticks low down near the basal bud, and gently twist and pull so that the stick comes away cleanly. You can keep picking rhubarb until July. After this the plants should be left to build up for next year.

Watch the plants for signs of the massive flowering stem. This is quite unmistakable, and should be removed quickly before it has a chance to grow; it should be cut or broken-off as low down as possible.

If you have first year roots of rhubarb, you should refrain from pulling sticks until the plants have had one full summer to become established.

MAY

"Who weeding slacketh,
good husbandrie lacketh."

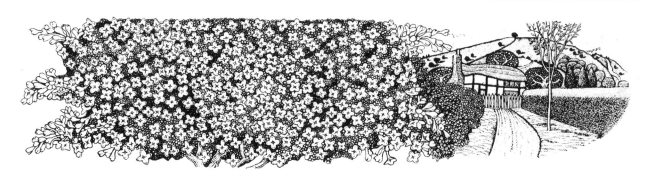

The asparagus is ready, and summer has arrived. May is a good month, almost invariably hot and bright, and the garden will need a lot of attention. The fine weather means that weeds will appear almost as fast as you can hoe them; also you will have to dig out by the roots large perennials like docks and thistles. As well as weeds, you will notice the first pests—blackfly particularly. Be ready for them.

Although May is a summer month, there is still a real chance of frost, so you must be prepared; young crops can still be damaged badly if they are attacked. At this time of year, fast-growing vegetables need water, so don't let the soil dry out, and do your watering in the cool of the morning or evening. This is another lazy job, like hoeing: it takes time—either with can or hose—and it will give you a chance to have a regular, close look at the state of the garden.

The seed-bed will have produced a good number of young plants, and it is worth doing some trade with friends or neighbours, exchanging your surplus plants for some different types. And as you keep up with your sowings, make sure your original plan is working. Be ready to make alterations, and above all think ahead.

Summary
1) *General work: clearing ground, the compost heap, hoeing, watering.*
2) *Sowing and planting: kales and savoys, French beans, runner beans,*

sweet corn, marrows, cucumber, brussels sprouts, potatoes.
3) *Thinning and successional sowings: lettuce, radish, turnip, beetroot, carrot, peas, parsnips, onions.*
4) *New crops: asparagus, spring cabbage, spinach.*
5) *Pests: blackfly, carrot fly, onion fly, cabbage root fly, turnip flea-beetle.*

General work

Clearing ground
As you finish up the winter and spring greens, clear the land and prepare it for new crops. It is not worth leaving the stumps of cabbages in the ground so that they can produce more leaves; there is no shortage of food from the garden at this time of year, and the ground will be needed for planting other crops. So put all the old and decaying leaves on the compost heap, and dig up the roots and stumps. These can either be burned or put to rot.

The compost heap
Keep building up the compost heap with all the old vegetable matter from the kitchen, coarse grass, annual weeds, leaves and so on. It's worth climbing on to the heap and treading it down; also the sides should be kept firm and tidy, if you have simply built the heap in one corner of the garden.

It is best to make a separate heap for grass cuttings. This should be allowed to rot for a whole year, and then the foul-smelling compost can be used for mulching crops. Never put grass cuttings on the land unless they are properly rotted.

Hoeing
At this time of year it is vital to hoe regularly between crops. This keeps down weeds and helps the soil to retain moisture—important in dry weather.

Watering
In dry weather it is important to water your crops regularly. Do this either in the morning or, better still, in the early evening. Watering in the middle of the day is pointless—the water evaporates too quickly—and it can harm the plants.

Water is valuable to all crops. 'Foliage' crops like spinach, cabbage and lettuce need plenty of water otherwise they wilt or bolt. Root crops and tubers also benefit, but if the roots are growing in dry soil and are suddenly heavily watered, this may cause them to swell so quickly that they split. Early potatoes should be watered as soon as the first shoots appear to encourage speedy growth of the tubers, while maincrop potatoes need most water after the tubers have begun to swell—this usually coincides with flowering.

Peas need plenty of water after the flowers have opened and the pods have begun to form, whereas runner beans need water as soon as they shoot. Different crops have different requirements: the main thing is to ensure that plants have enough water, and it is worth looking at your soil occasionally, not on the surface, but an inch or two below. You may be surprised to find that it is bone dry; in that case you must water more thoroughly.

Sowing and planting

Kales and savoys
Both of these can be sown in the seed-bed during the month. They will be ready for cropping in early winter and through until the spring. Sow the seeds in $\frac{1}{2}$in drills and thin the seedlings before transplanting in July.

May

French beans

Although you can sow these as early as the end of April in some areas, I always like to plant them in early May. They thrive better, and provide a useful crop between broad beans and runner beans. The ground should have been deeply dug in the winter, and a few days before sowing it should be broken up to a fine tilth. Take out drills 2in deep and water them a few hours before sowing the seeds 4-6in apart; the drills themselves should be 18in apart. Once the plants have germinated, they will need regular hoeing and watering.

Make a second sowing three weeks after the first.

Runner beans

You should decide early in the year where you are going to grow runner beans, and whether you want the dwarf or climbing variety. I, personally, would choose the climbers every time, because runner beans grow very fast and have a great deal of foliage, and the dwarf varieties can become unwieldy. Picking dwarf runners is difficult and frustrating, pods tend to be crushed underfoot and flowers damaged. Of course, the climbers need a frame to climb up—poles, trellis work or any improvised structure that will stand the weight of the plants and will not be blown down by strong winds. Climbing runners are easy to pick, and the flowers stand out—a colourful invitation to insects.

All types of runner bean need to be grown in well dug, rich soil—light rather than heavy—and the plants need plenty of sun; the rows should run north to south. If you dug out trenches earlier in the year, more well-rotted refuse can be put in now and they can gradually be filled; do this in stages, treading down the soil firmly as you go.

You are now ready to sow. But watch out for frost—the greatest enemy of the runner bean. In most areas, it is best to delay sowing until the end of May or even the beginning of June. If you intend to grow the beans against poles or stakes, sow in a double row. Take out two drills, 1ft apart, and 2-3in deep, and sow the seeds singly at 6in intervals. You will probably need to thin out every alternate seedling in due course. It is a good idea to sow a few extra at the end of the row; these can be used to fill any gaps where the seeds do not germinate.

Once the seedlings have been thinned, the rows can be hoed and the poles or stakes put in. Use canes or wooden poles formed into an arch, with

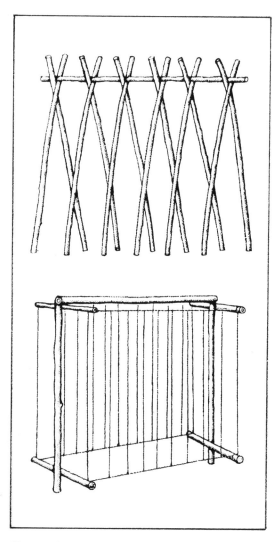

Runner beans can be trained to grow up poles, against trellis-work or netting and even against walls using a frame, poles or hop string.

a supporting pole tied along the length of the arch where the poles meet. If you are short of space, you can grow the beans in a circle, and there are several types of structure that you can buy to deal with this arrangement, but they are laborious to set up, and are not as sturdy as they seem, particularly in exposed spots.

When you are staking beans in the normal way, you should make sure that each plant has a pole about 3in from it and that the poles themselves are tall enough; they need to be 7-8ft high to be really effective.

Whatever sort of structure you decide to use, the main points to remember are that it should be tall and sturdy. Don't be afraid to improvise with any odds and ends that may be hidden away in your shed or garage.

At first, the plants may need a little assistance and encouragement to climb; once a runner is long enough it can be loosely tied to the pole. But make sure that you do not damage the runner by tying it too tight.

Sweet corn

It is possible to grow sweet corn successfully, but only in warm districts. It needs a very sunny, but sheltered spot and a rich soil. On an exposed, windy allotment it is less likely to grow well.

You can sow the seeds in open ground in May. They are quite hardy and germinate within a few days if the weather is good. As the plants are pollinated by wind, it is best to arrange them in a block rather than a long row; you can do this by making a number of quite short rows 2ft apart. Take out drills 1in deep and put two seeds at 18in intervals. When the seeds have germinated, remove the weakest, leaving single plants. Once the plants have started to grow they will need plenty of water and may need some support. A little earth built up and firmed round the base of the plants will usually prevent them from keeling over in the wind.

Marrows

An easy and worthwhile crop, and you can choose between trailing and bush marrows. As a rule, trailing marrows are suited to growing on heaps or raised beds, while bush marrows, being more contained and manageable, are best grown in open ground. I prefer trailing marrows grown on a heap of well-rotted manure or compost, although this method is now frowned upon by some gardeners who think too much about cleanliness and hygiene in the garden.

Trailing marrows: If you are going to grow trailing marrows, you should start to build a raised bed early in the year. Use well-rotted manure, decaying leaves and greenstuff, and tread and compress the heap as it progresses. Finally level off the surface and put about 3in of good soil on top of it. Sow a couple of seeds at various sites on the heap 1in deep. It doesn't matter where you actually sow, provided that there is sufficient space between each site; 2-3ft is a useful distance.

Bush marrows: It is best to select a site in open ground where the soil has been deeply dug and manured. Take out a drill 1in deep and sow a couple of seeds at 3ft intervals.

After sowing, both types can be dealt with in the same way. It is a good idea to cover the seed sites with an inverted jam jar, which can be left there until the seedlings are showing. Remove the weaker of the two plants and cover the other one at night with the jam jar until it is established.

Watering of marrows is very important. The plants won't thrive if deprived of a regular and large amount of water. Either make a small depression or pit alongside each plant, or sink a small flower pot into the soil and fill this regularly.

Courgettes (zucchini) are sown and

cultivated in exactly the same way as marrows and are worth growing as well. Their tender skins, lack of pith or seeds and their special flavour make them excellent summer vegetables.

Marrows and courgettes may be attacked by the cucumber mosaic virus, which causes stunted growth, mottling of the leaves and distortion of the marrows themselves. There is no remedy for this except to remove the infected plants and burn them immediately. Slugs are another problem as are woodlice and these may be trapped under the half skins of an orange or grapefruit (see p. 22).

Cucumber

Outdoor cucumbers can be grown rather like marrows, except that the plants are usually trained on a frame or wire netting. A good crop is very dependent on the weather. Often the plants start well, flower and then deteriorate.

For sowing outdoors you must get a variety of 'ridge cucumber'—so called because the plants are usually grown on ridges, or mounds of manure and soil. Other varieties, suitable for growing in greenhouses or hot frames, are no good outdoors. Like marrows, cucumbers need a rich soil, plenty of sun, plenty of manure and organic matter in the soil, and plenty of water.

In average or heavy soils, the easiest plan is to build a ridge. First, put down a layer of *fresh* manure. This is important since it will provide heat as well as nutrients. Cucumbers like a warm root run and this is best supplied with fresh manure. Cover the mound with 4-6in of good soil, which can be firmed down and formed into a bed for sowing. Make a drill 1in deep and sow the seeds on edge, in pairs, and 1ft apart if they are going to be trained on netting. (If they are going to trail then the seeds should be 2ft apart.) Once the seeds have germinated, and the first leaves have formed, they should be thinned leaving only the stronger of each pair.

The plants should be watered whenever necessary, and next month they will need to be trained and stopped.

Plant the young cabbages and other brassicas in holes large enough to accommodate the roots comfortably, and firm the plants well with a dibber as shown, or with the toe of your boot.

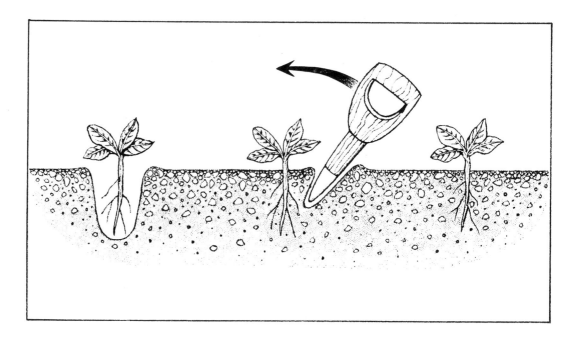

May

Brussels sprouts

Young plants, either raised from seed, or purchased, can be planted out at the end of the month. The night before you decide to plant, water the plants in the seed-bed. Choose a site in the garden where the soil was well-dug and manured at the beginning of the year, or a place where winter crops other than brassicas grew. The ground should be forked and firmed by treading.

Mark out rows with a line and take out drills with a hoe. Make holes for each plant with a trowel or a dibber, water the soil if it is at all dry, and then set the plants firmly and deep into each hole. There should be 2ft between each one, and 2½ft between the rows. Once the plants are in, give them another watering—the drill will help to direct the water.

Cabbages, kale and *winter heading broccoli* sown in late March or early April should be dealt with in the same way.

Potatoes

If you still have some seed potatoes, they should all be planted this month.

Thinning and successional sowings

Lettuce

Continue with lettuce sowing, and aim to sow a few seeds every 2-3 weeks depending on your needs. At the same time start to thin and/or transplant the more established seedlings; they should be thinned first to 3in apart and finally to 9in apart.

Radish

Since radishes benefit from a fast growing season it is wise to sow a short row every 2-3 weeks. The seedlings should be thinned early to leave the radishes 3in apart.

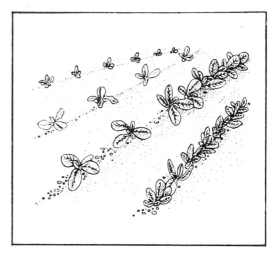

Gently thin rows of seedlings, such as carrots, lettuce, etc., in several stages until you have single plants at regular intervals.

Turnips

Make the last sowing of turnips this month before the weather becomes too hot; they will be ready for pulling in about 2 months.

Beetroot

Sow another row of beetroot towards the end of the month. This will give you a good supply through the winter, particularly if many of the early sowings are eaten young during the summer.

The first sowings may need to be thinned in the second half of the month. Use the larger thinnings in salads or for pickling. Eventually the roots should be 6in apart and can then be left to grow until the autumn.

Carrots

Sow the last of the maincrop carrots this month.

Rows of early carrots can now be thinned. If they were sown in groups, the seedlings should be reduced to single plants; if sown in a continuous row, they should be thinned out evenly along the row. The very first thinnings will probably be too small to use, but before long, some delicious young carrots can be pulled. You must firm the soil and rake it around the remaining carrots to prevent the carrot fly from laying its eggs in the loose soil around the top of the roots. Don't leave thinnings or odd leaves lying around the garden, as the scent attracts this destructive pest. Early carrots should be thinned so that they are finally about 5in apart.

Peas

Sow more maincrop peas this month. Make the new sowings as soon as the previous sowing has germinated and has begun to show.

Parsnips

Thin out the groups of young parsnips, leaving a single strong plant at each site. Make sure you do not disturb this plant when you pull out the weaker seedlings.

Onions

If you planted onion seeds in March, they can be thinned this month, and the thinnings used as salad onions. They are first thinned to ½in apart and finally to leave the onions 6in apart. Don't disturb the remaining seedlings, and firm the soil around them after thinning.

New crops

As well as the young carrots, onions and beetroot that may be large enough to eat from thinnings, there are several crops which can be picked this month.

Asparagus

May is the month for asparagus. The shoots or sticks can be cut provided that the plants are at least three years old. You should aim to take shoots when they are 6-8in long: too short, and they will not be sufficiently well-developed; too long, and they are likely to be stringy and bitter.

Cut the sticks below ground level. Scrape a little soil away from the base of

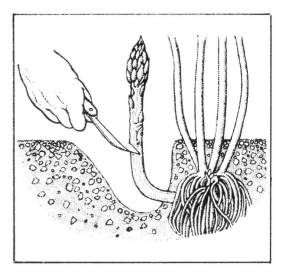

Cut sticks of asparagus carefully. Use a very sharp knife and make a slanting downward cut through the stem below the level of the soil.

the shoot and make a downwards slanting cut into the white part. Be careful not to sever any other shoots or to plunge the knife in too deep so that it cuts the actual roots of the asparagus.

The most difficult part of cutting asparagus is judging the rate of growth of the crop so that you can make regular pickings and cut enough sticks for a good feed each time. They should be cooked and eaten the day you cut them. Trim the sticks so that they are all roughly the same length, wash them and tie them in a bundle. Put this, upright, into a saucepan of boiling water, so that the stems can cook while the delicate tips are moistened and softened by steam. At the last minute, when the sticks are cooked, you may need to plunge the tips into the water for a short while to finish them.

Serve the asparagus straight away with hot melted butter. It has a short season, so enjoy it now, and don't be tempted to save or preserve the crop by bottling or freezing.

Spring cabbage

By now, the spring cabbages should

have hearted up well, and can be cut when needed. They sometimes mature quite late if the spring weather is bad, and if this is the case, they can be used well into June. Dig out the stumps after you have cut the cabbages.

Spinach

If you made an early sowing of round-seeded spinach, the first leaves can be picked this month. A few small pickings at this stage will help to stimulate the growth of the plants. Don't pick too heavily at first; take a few of the outer leaves from several plants, and never strip one plant completely.

At this time of year, the leaves and leaf stalks can be cooked together—this gives the spinach an extra succulent taste. The simplest way of cooking is to wash the spinach and put it, still wet, into a saucepan with a little salt, but no water, then boil it briskly. When it is tender, it should be strained well and buttered. The number of uses for spinach is almost endless: it is the perfect vegetable to go with simply grilled fish, it goes well with eggs, it makes marvellous soup, and I often use it in Oriental cooking as a bed for thick spicy dishes.

The tender growing tops of broad bean plants can become infested with blackfly. The tops should be pinched off.

Pests

You should be on the lookout for the first threatening pests in May. It is always best to be prepared, to watch and act quickly as soon as you see the first signs of infestation. And always work to discourage pests altogether.

Blackfly

These are usually the first to appear. They cluster and multiply at the top of broad bean plants, around the sweet flowering shoots. Autumn sown and early spring sown broad beans are less vulnerable than later sowings, but as a precaution you should nip out the soft

tips of all plants while they are in flower and the young beans are just beginning to form. These tips should be burned immediately.

When you do notice the fly, nip out the tips and also spray the plants with a soap solution. You can make this up by dissolving a handful of *soft soap* in a little hot water; dilute this to 2 gallons with clear water, (the solution should be slightly warm) and then spray thoroughly on the plants.

If blackfly is not dealt with, it can completely ruin a broad bean crop, and it may also spread to French beans as well.

Carrot fly

The problem here is that the carrot fly lays its eggs around the surface of the roots, and the grubs burrow and eat their way into the carrots. As I mentioned earlier, the danger is greatest during thinning. The fly is attracted by the scent of the plants and the disturbed soil is an ideal site for its eggs. So firm the soil after thinning, and don't leave any thinnings or stray leaves scattered on the ground. These precautions are reasonably effective, but if your plants are infested, a dusting of naphthalene hoed in along the rows will help to keep the flies at bay.

Onion fly

If your young onions start to wilt and turn yellow, it is likely that they have been attacked by the grubs of the onion fly. The first job is to pull up all the affected plants. Then you can either spray with a soap solution like broad beans, or scatter a mixture of paraffin and sand alongside the rows; the smell of this discourages the fly, as does naphthalene. An old idea is to grow parsley between the rows of onions.

The onion fly, like the carrot fly, tends to be attracted by the scent inevitably produced during thinning. So be careful. If the fly is established, it is best to change the site next year even if this means a lot of extra work.

Cabbage root fly

Young cabbages may be attacked by the grubs of the cabbage root fly, which destroys the roots, causing wilting and yellowing of the leaves. If you sprinkle naphthalene along the rows soon after planting out this will protect the roots of the young plants. Any plants that are attacked should be pulled up and burnt.

Turnip flea-beetle

This beetle attacks young turnips and also young brassica seedlings; it nibbles the leaves. In this case the plants can be dusted with old soot, but it must be old, or it will scorch the leaves.

JUNE

"Good gardener mine,
make garden fine."

For the next couple of months, the garden will look at its best. All signs of winter are gone, and, with plenty of crops coming to fruition, the vegetable patch should be luxuriant. Later it may seem rather parched, but in June it is a satisfying sight. Rows of broad beans ready for picking, lettuces and other salad vegetables that can be gathered almost every day for light lunches and suppers, recognizable rows of green-leaved root crops and potatoes growing visibly each day—not long now till the first home-grown earlies.

Looking at the garden, it is easy to think that all the work is finished; you can be deceived into believing that it will continue to produce food without any more assistance or encouragement. So look more closely: you will see weeds among your seedlings, pests and caterpillars lurking around the crops. And check the soil, it may look all right, but beneath the surface it may be dangerously dry.

There is always work to be done. Of course June brings the first pickings of the big summer crops, but unless you look after the land, you may soon lose more than you gain.

Summary
1) *General work: weeding, watering, mulching.*
2) *Sowing and planting: swedes, endive, celeriac, celery, brassicas, tomatoes.*
3) *Successional sowing and thinning.*
4) *Gathering: broad beans, potatoes, salad crops, spinach, asparagus.*

June

General work

It is important to keep up with regular chores in the garden.

Hoe regularly between all your crops. Disturb the tiny annuals like groundsel before they are established, and be sure to dig out any big perennials.

Watering: as crops like peas and beans come into flower and start to form pods, they will need plenty of water. It will not hurt to give them a soaking every evening. The same applies to early potatoes. In fact no crop should be allowed to dry out at this time of year, otherwise you may be in real danger of losing the whole lot.

Mulching: crops like peas and beans will benefit from a mulching of decayed grass cuttings, which should be forked thickly around the rows. This helps the soil to retain moisture and also tends to keep down weeds.

Stake and tie any crops that are in danger of being damaged by the wind. When broad beans are at their full height and are heavy with pods, they are very vulnerable. So support them by putting a stake at each corner of the rows and wind twine around them. This will enclose and support the plants. Check your pea sticks and bean poles to see that they are secure.

Finally keep your eyes open for pests and signs of disease in the crops.

Sowing and planting

Swedes
Swedes are very hardy and should stand up to the worst frosts, so they may be more worthwhile than winter turnips. Early June is the usual time for sowing, and this will give you a good winter crop. If you want swedes in the autumn, you should sow them in April, though they will be less resistant to mildew.

The main requirement for swedes is deeply dug moist soil. Make drills 1in deep and sow the seeds thinly in continuous rows, which should be 15in apart. The seedlings will need to be thinned so that single plants stand 1ft apart.

Endive
This is one of the best winter vegetables. It is very crisp, and its slightly bitter taste seems much more suited to winter salads than ordinary lettuce. Seeds sown in late June will produce endives ready for use in the autumn. If you want them in the summer, they can be sown in April, but it is probably better to wait until later in the year when there is less in the garden.

Prepare the ground as for lettuces (see page 41), choosing a spot that has been well dug to allow good root growth. Sow the seeds in $\frac{1}{2}$in drills, and thin the plants in two stages so that they are finally 1ft apart. About 3 weeks before the endives are needed they will have to be blanched; this will be about 9 weeks after sowing at this time of year, and slightly longer if the seeds are sown later.

It is worth mentioning that the leaves of young endives can be used in the summer, cooked like spinach; blanching is only necessary to produce the special leaves for salads.

Celeriac
Seeds sown in April can now be moved to a permanent spot in the garden. It is best to plant them in drills 2in deep made with a hoe. They need to be planted quite shallowly, making sure they are firm, but using a deeper drill makes watering easier and more effective in dry soils. The plants should be set 1ft apart in drills 18in apart.

During the summer celeriac needs a lot of water, and regular hoeing. It is also advisable to nip off any side-shoots as they appear. The plants will be ready for use in October or November when the swollen base of the stem stops growing.

Celery
Both ordinary (trench) celery and self-blanching celery can be raised from seeds outdoors in April if the weather is good, but they are more reliable if started in a greenhouse and gradually hardened off. Alternatively you can buy young plants and put them out in June, which is the best month for celery planting. You should plant when the celery is about 6in high.

Trench celery: the important point with this crop is that it has to be blanched. This means planting out in a deep trench and progressively earthing up until the whole plant is covered except for the leaves. You should have dug and prepared a suitable trench some time ago (see p. 38).

The night before you intend to move the plants give them a good watering. Next day lift them out with a trowel making sure that there is a ball of moist soil clinging to the roots, and plant along the centre of the trench, 8in apart. Water the plants well during their growing season, but be careful to keep water out of the centre of the celery as this can cause browning and decay.

Once the plants are established and have grown a few inches, they can be earthed up. This is a job for later in the year.

Self-blanching celery: this crop has advantages and disadvantages. It does not need to be grown in trenches and does not require earthing up. This saves work, but on the other hand the celery is not hardy and is liable to be damaged by frost.

The ground should be prepared and manured as for trench celery—but no trench needs to be dug. Self-blanching celery is best grown in blocks rather than rows. This arrangement gives the plants support and protection as well as helping the blanching process. Set the plants 9in apart each way using a trowel as before. They also need plenty of water.

Brassicas: cauliflowers, cabbages, etc.
Spring-sown cabbages, cauliflowers and brussels sprouts should be transplanted from the seed-bed to the main plot, as the ground is ready.

A few hours before planting out, water the seed-bed well. The young plants should be lifted carefully with a trowel with the moist soil clinging to the roots. Mark out drills and make holes for the plants at the correct spacing for each type:

Cabbages: plants 18in apart; rows 2ft apart
Cauliflowers: plants 2ft apart; rows 2½ft apart
Brussels sprouts: plants 2ft apart; rows 2½ft apart

If the soil is dry, water the holes before planting, and give the water time to soak into the soil. Then set the plants into the holes, so that the stems are covered up to the level of the first leaf, and firm them. You can do this, first with your hands, then by pushing the dibber into the soil alongside each plant, and carefully pressing it towards the plant.

Once the plants are in, give them another watering. The drill and the dibber holes will help to direct the water.

Tomatoes
Unless you have a good greenhouse, the easiest way of growing tomatoes outdoors is to buy plants in early June and put them out straight away. When you buy plants look for those grown in pots, rather than cramped in boxes; they should be about 9in high, sturdy with thick stems and dark green leaves. Leggy plants with light green leaves will be no good.

Tomatoes like a sunny spot out of the wind, and soil that has been deeply dug with plenty of leaf mould and wood ash added to it. Stable manure, if used, should be well rotted and put at the very bottom of the bed. If near the surface it will cause the plants to grow too quickly, producing a mass of foliage but no fruit. The best position is along a fence or wall that faces south or west. Failing that, the tomatoes can be grown in the open in rows running from north to south, to get full sun.

Plant the tomatoes in either the first or second week of the month, depending on the weather. Water the plants in their boxes or pots an hour or so before transplanting. Make planting holes with a trowel at 18in intervals along the row. If you are putting the tomatoes next to a fence or wall, the holes should be about 6in away from the wall, and they must be large enough to take the plant and the ball of soil attached to the roots. If possible, plants in pots should be removed intact with their solid network of roots and soil. Set each plant into a hole and work and firm the soil around it with the trowel handle until the whole root system is just covered; you should then have a depression or trough around each plant which will help watering later on. Give the plants a good soaking once they are in the soil.

Tomatoes must be staked, this can be done before planting or immediately after, but care must then be taken to avoid damaging the roots. The stakes should be about 5ft long and must be strong. They are pushed into the soil about 3in behind each plant. Tie each stem of the plant to the stake with twine or raffia. Do this carefully. The string should be looped around the stake and then tied loosely around the plant, to give it room for growth. As the plant develops, more ties will have to be made.

Tomatoes need quite a lot of attention. They need regular watering, and you should watch for any signs of side shoots. It is essential to remove these as soon as possible, to keep the plant as a

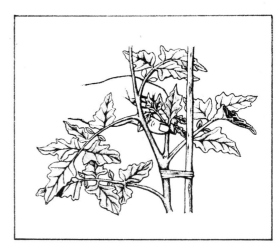

Pick out the side shoots of tomato plants when they appear in the leaf axils to leave the strong central stem.

single stem. These shoots appear in the leaf axils—that is the angle between the leaf stalk and the main stem.
Bush tomatoes: these can be planted as above, but they do not need to be staked, and the side shoots are allowed to develop without interference. It is a good idea to put a bed of straw beneath the plants to prevent the lower fruit from being spoiled.

Successional sowing and thinning

Continue to sow, thin and pick rows of young salad vegetables like lettuces and radishes. If you find that your lettuces are bolting, don't simply pull them up and throw them on the rubbish heap—they can be used. The leaves can be stripped and used for lettuce soup, while the succulent inner portions of the stems can be preserved in thick sugar syrup with ginger.

Radishes also can be used when they have apparently outgrown themselves. If you leave them in the soil and allow them to flower and eventually go to seed, the odd-looking green pods can be harvested and pickled. These radish pods are a good and interesting

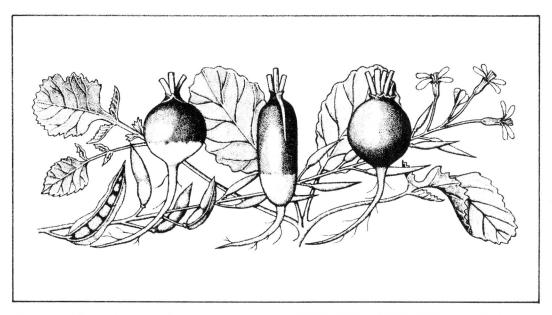

There are two main types of summer radish—one spherical, the other long and cylindrical. The pods that form if the plants are allowed to go to seed are useful for pickling.

addition to winter salads. Their taste is not at all like that of a cultivated vegetable. They can be either chopped up or left whole.

The thinnings from carrots, beetroot and onions will now be large enough to use in the kitchen. Young carrots can be washed and eaten raw in salads, or they can be cooked and dressed with some melted butter and a little sugar; they are some of the most delicious of summer vegetables—a real treat. Beetroot will be large enough to pull and use for salads or pickling, and onion thinnings will now be ideal for 'spring onions'.

Some people may want to make a second sowing of French and runner beans. This is certainly a good idea if you want to harvest and store the seeds, or salt the beans, also if you intend to store a large quantity in a freezer. Normally these beans produce heavy crops over a fairly long period, so unless you have a special use for the extra amount, be content with the earlier sowing.

Gathering

Broad beans
There should be plenty of broad beans to pick during June. Autumn sown plants will be ready first, followed a couple of weeks later by the first spring sowings. Before picking, it is best to feel the pods to test if the beans inside have developed properly; often they look large, but the beans are tiny. Pick regularly, and don't let the beans get too big to begin with. Later you can leave them, and store the seeds. But now you need the best for eating. The massive piles of empty pods left after shelling the beans can be taken out and put on the compost heap. Incidentally it is worth cooking a few broad beans whole, in their pods, they need to be very small, and can be sliced like runner beans. This is a bit extravagant, but delicious if you can spare the beans.

Potatoes
By the end of the month you may be able to dig the first new potatoes, depending on when you planted the tubers. But don't be too eager to lift them; give them plenty of time to develop. Wait until the leaves have started to turn yellow and then dig one root to see how large the

June

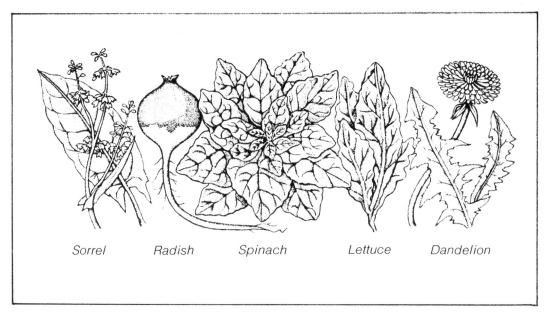

Sorrel Radish Spinach Lettuce Dandelion

You can gather many salad vegetables at this time of year: thinnings from carrot and beetroot, as well as radishes, young dandelion, sorrel and spinach leaves and, of course, lettuce.

tubers are. And look at the skins; if they are flaky, and tear easily, the potatoes have not completed their growth, and should be left.

Use a long-tined fork for lifting potatoes. Work along the row and slide the fork downwards at an angle at the base of the ridge. Lever the fork down as far as it will go and lift the complete plant, if possible, holding the tops with one hand. This should minimize the danger of spearing the potatoes. However, if you do damage any, use them up straight away. As you dig along the row unload each plant into the space left by the previous plant, so you are effectively digging and turning over the land. Unless you are going to use the potatoes straight away, they should be left on the ground for an hour or so to dry out if the weather is good. The object of

this is to dry the skins before storing.

All the tops can be collected and either put with other refuse to rot, or burned to produce valuable potash which can be dug into the soil where needed.

Salad crops
Continue to use lettuces, radishes, spring onions, young beetroot as well as carrot thinnings.

Spinach
Spinach should be well established and pickings can be made regularly. This stimulates the plant to produce more leaves, but remember to take off any very large or damaged leaves.

Asparagus
You can continue to cut sticks of asparagus until the middle of June if a lot of thick succulent shoots are still being produced. Normally, however, they start to become spindly now and should be left to grow unhindered until the autumn.

JULY

"The pleasure is fine,
the profit is thine."

July can be your busiest month. Although nearly all the crops have been planted and are growing well, there is still a great deal to do if you want to obtain both pleasure *and* profit from your food garden.

In theory, July should be the hottest and driest month of the year, but it seldom is. However, you should be ready to deal with the effects of drought and very hot weather—not only extra watering and hoeing, but also fast growing crops and regular pickings to keep pace with the plants. July is also the time to start organizing and controlling crops like tomatoes, celery and cucumbers, which will be ready in the next couple of months.

These tasks are part of the pleasure of the garden. But at this time of year it is the harvesting which is the most pleasurable aspect of all: collecting broad beans and peas, picking salad vegetables, lifting shallots—the first plantings of the year, and now a cluster of new bulbs with dried yellow leaves. And this pleasure is part of the profit too. It is not only the money saved, but it is also the fact that you have actually *produced* which is the real profit. The evidence of this will now be filling your kitchen and store house.

Summary
1) *Looking after crops: brussels sprouts, cauliflowers, runner beans, tomatoes, marrows, cucumbers, celery, onions and shallots.*
2) *Sowing and planting: spinach, kale (hungry gap), parsley, kohl-rabi, leeks, savoy cabbages, sprouting broccoli, kale, winter brassicas.*

3) *Gathering, lifting and picking: broad beans, peas, French beans, potatoes, globe artichokes, shallots, herbs and herb drying, kohl-rabi.*

Looking after crops

This month a number of crops will need special attention.

Brussels sprouts
Sprouts planted earlier in the year will need to be earthed up and the soil made firm around the base of the stems. This will give the plants some extra support and help to prevent them becoming very tall and spindly, which can happen if the soil is loose and shallow.

Cauliflowers
One of the disadvantages of cauliflowers is that all the plants from one sowing tend to produce curds at about the same time; so you may suddenly find you have an abundance of cauliflowers which need cutting. If

Protect cauliflowers in the summer by bending the outer leaves over the curds.

you cannot use all of them or share them with friends, they can be protected by bending and tying the large outer leaves over the curds; this shields the curd from the sun, and stops it running to flower.

Runner beans
When the runner beans have wound their way to the top of the poles, they will need to be 'stopped'. This can be done by simply pinching out the growing points, to encourage the plant to divert its energy into forming pods. At this stage the plants should be watered regularly and a mulch of old grass cuttings will help to keep the soil moist.

Tomatoes
As the tomatoes grow, continue tying and supporting the stems, and pinching out any side-shoots that appear. Watch the plants carefully because at a certain stage they will also have to be 'stopped'. As the trusses (or flower stems) form, small tomatoes will begin to appear after the flowers have been fertilized. Each plant should be stopped when it has formed 4, or at the most, 5 trusses. This will probably happen next month. There is no point in allowing the plants to form too many trusses since the tomatoes would be very small.

Marrows
Marrows sown last month should be established by now. The protective pots or jars can be removed and the seedlings reduced to a single strong plant at each site. From now on the plants must be watered regularly—using the 'well' alongside each plant—and you should watch for the first flowers.

Cucumbers
Ridge cucumbers will need to be trained. When each plant has formed two pairs of leaves, it must be stopped, by pinching out the growing point. This encourages the plant to form side-shoots. The plants produce both male and female flowers, but the fruit

are borne only on the female, and develop without fertilization. You should have one fruit on each side-shoot, so pinch out the growing point of each shoot one leaf beyond the tiny cucumber.

The plants can either be tied, and encouraged to grow up a wire frame, or they can be left to trail; if this is the case, some straw should be put under the fruit to protect them from the soil. Water the plants regularly, and it will encourage growth if they are given some liquid manure as well (see page 23).

Celery
Both trench and self-blanching celery should be established. Watch out for any side-shoots or suckers that appear, and remove them immediately otherwise they will weaken the plants. Dust the leaves with old soot; this helps growth and also tends to discourage pests like celery fly. Water the plants regularly making sure you do not splash any water into the celery hearts, otherwise they may rot.

Be ready to earth up trench celery once the plants have made a few inches' growth. This may not be necessary until next month.

Onions and shallots
Both onions and shallots should be watched for any signs of running to seed. As soon as small pods are spotted, they must be nipped off, otherwise the stem will harden and the onion bulbs will not swell properly. If you notice any onions that have these thick or hard stems, either squash and bend the stem, or make a vertical cut into it with a penknife just above the bulb itself; this will help to stop sap flow. Any onions like this should be used early, as they will not store well. As the bulbs begin to swell, it will help if you scrape away the soil from the sides of each bulb with a hoe, making sure that you do not disturb the roots. In dry

weather the onions should be watered.

Shallots will almost be ready for lifting. The stems will start to droop and turn yellow and they should be bent over to the ground. At the end of the month they can be lifted (see p. 70).

As well as these special jobs, you should keep up with general hoeing, weeding and watering when this is necessary.

Sowing and planting

Spinach
July is a good time to sow perpetual spinach. This is a hardy and useful crop which will provide pickings through the autumn and winter. Sow it like summer spinach, in 1in deep drills, and sow the seeds very thinly in a short row; later thin the plants to 3in, and finally 6in apart.

Kale (Hungry Gap)
This variety of kale can be grown from seed for use in April, and it is particularly useful in cold districts. Sow the seeds in ground that was manured for an early crop. This kale has the advantage of not needing to be transplanted. Simply sow the seeds in drills ½in deep, and thin the plants so that they are finally 18in apart where they can remain through the winter.

Parsley
It may be worth making a late sowing this month to provide fresh supplies through the winter. Dried parsley is not really worth attempting—as it bears no resemblance to the fresh herb, and cannot be used like fresh parsley.

Make a small sowing in ½in drills as before.

Successional sowings
Make another sowing of turnips for winter use; also sow more lettuce, late carrots and kohl-rabi.

July

Leeks

July is the best month for planting out leeks sown earlier in the year. They will be ready for lifting in the late autumn and through the winter. Leeks need a rich, deeply dug soil and plenty of moisture, so plant them in ground that was well-manured last winter, or where a crop has been cleared and the land dug and manured in the spring.

If the seed-bed is dry then it is a good idea to soak it well a few hours before lifting the young leek seedlings with a fork. It makes lifting easier and also means that soil adheres to the roots, which is useful when planting out. Mark out rows on the main plot 15in apart, and plant the leeks at 9in intervals. It is worth trimming the leaves so that each plant is about 8in long.

The actual planting is rather important if you want long stemmed, thick leeks. Make holes at least 6in deep with a dibber and drop a leek carefully into each hole so that it touches the bottom. Don't fill with soil, but merely pour water into the holes; this will draw enough soil down into the hole to anchor the roots. As you water and hoe the crop, more soil will find its way into the holes. After planting, only the tops of the leaves should be showing above the soil.

Once the plants are in, they will need to be watered regularly, and a feed of liquid manure every fortnight will help growth considerably.

Savoy cabbages

These can be planted anywhere on the plot, but grow best where the soil is rich and has been well dug. The seeds sown in April in the seed-bed can be transplanted into rows marked out 2ft apart, and there should be 18in between each plant. They will be ready in November, but you should wait until they have been exposed to frost before cutting any.

Sprouting broccoli

These can be treated rather like brussels sprout plants. They like rich, moist and very firm soil—so you may need to tread the soil before planting them out. Set them 20in apart in rows 2ft apart, and plant them so that the stems are covered up to the level of the lower leaves.

Kale

Again, a rich, deeply dug and firm soil with plenty of moisture is the best site for curly kale. The plants are very bushy and need plenty of space. They should be planted in staggered rows, so that there is 2ft between the plants in any direction. Lift the young plants from the seed-bed with a trowel so that soil is attached to the roots, and plant firmly like cabbages. Water the planting hole first if necessary, and cover the stems up to the first leaves. It is important to water and hoe regularly.

Winter cabbages and late cauliflowers can also be planted out as before (see page 55). With these crops it is vital that you keep a watch for pests of all kinds. The main offenders at this time of year

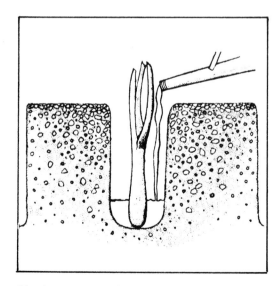

The best way to plant leeks is to make the holes with a dibber and drop in the young plants. Don't fill the holes or firm the soil around the plants as this will happen automatically with watering.

are caterpillars on the leaves. The egg masses should be crushed and the grubs can either be picked off by hand or sprayed with a salt solution (1 handful of salt to a bucket of water). Salt solution should be used as soon as any sign of caterpillars is seen as it is only harmful to the very small grubs. Greenfly can be treated in a similar fashion.

Gathering, lifting and picking

Broad beans
There should be plenty of broad beans during July. If you want to save some of the beans for next year's seed, leave the pods on the plant until the tops of the leaves start to turn black. If the weather is bad, pull up the plants and suspend them from the ceiling of the shed or some other dry place until the pods have turned yellow. Then remove the beans and spread them out on a tray to dry; pack them in a jar or brown paper bag and keep them in a cool, dry place away from the light until they are needed.

Broad bean plants that have been stripped of all their pods can be cut down to ground level. It is a good idea, however, to leave the roots in the soil for as long as possible as the root nodules put valuable nitrogen back into the soil. These stumps can be dug out when the ground needs to be cleared.

Peas
If you waited until April before sowing peas, you should pick the first pods in July. The main rule with peas is to pick them before they get too large. Don't wait until the pods are bulging, and be careful how you remove them. If you try to pull them from the plant, you may damage the stems. Use both hands—one steadying the main stem, the other holding the pod—or nip them off with a pair of scissors

French beans
These should be picked rather like peas, that is young and regularly. The best French beans are pencil-thin with no signs of bulging seeds. Once they become hard and stringy, they are not worth eating as a fresh vegetable, although they do have other uses, in soups for instance. Once your broad beans are finished, French beans will be the main bean crop until the runner beans are ready for picking.

Search through the rows carefully, collecting all the pods that are the right

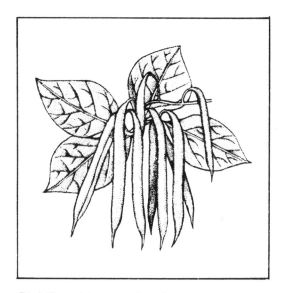

Pick French beans when the pods are a few inches long and very thin.

size, and harvest them like peas. Try not to leave any to grow too large, unless you intend to harvest and dry the beans later.

These first pickings should be eaten simply—cooked whole until they are just soft and dressed with fresh parsley and garlic butter.

Potatoes
By July there should be plenty of earlies ready for lifting. Because these taste so delicious when dug straight from the ground, only dig when you need potatoes for your next meal or two. But it

is not a good idea to leave potatoes in the ground for too long after the foliage has died off. They are prey to any number of grubs and insects which live in the soil.

Globe artichokes

The globes—or half-opened flower heads—will be ready for cutting in early July. Don't wait until they are fully opened. Cut the heads with a few inches of stem, using secateurs. After you have taken the main head from each plant, it will produce side-shoots each bearing a smaller globe; these can be cut when they are the right size.

Before cooking the artichokes, cut off the stem and also a small portion of the top of each globe, and pull off any damaged or old 'leaves'. Then wash well and cook in salted water until the 'leaves' are soft and can be peeled off easily. Remove them one by one, dip them in melted butter, draw them between your teeth, and eat the soft inner portion. When the leaves have all been dealt with, scoop out and discard the whiskers from the fleshy base, and finally eat this.

Shallots

Once the leaves of the shallots have turned yellow and dried up, the plants

Lift the clusters of shallots when the stems are dry and yellow.

have finished growing. Lift the clusters of bulbs with a fork, rub off any excess soil, separate the bulbs and spread them to dry outside if the weather is good. Once the outer skins have dried, the shallots can be stored. Remove any remnants of the dried tops and pack the bulbs in trays or shallow boxes in a dry place. A few choice bulbs should be put aside for next year's planting.

Shallots can be used in cooking, like whole small onions, but they are really best made into pickled 'onions' during August and September.

Kohl-rabi

Spring sowings of kohl-rabi will be ready for lifting this month. Use them when they are the size of turnips. Dig up the plants, strip off the leaves, and peel and cook the swollen stems like turnips.

As well as the above crops, there are others which can be eaten this month: cabbages and cauliflowers, young summer carrots, turnips, beetroot, lettuces, radishes and so on.

Herbs and herb drying

The best time to dry herbs is when they are just coming into flower. Of course this will vary depending on the species, but most plants will be at this stage between June and August. The plants' leaves are full of a high concentration of aromatic oils and so have the best flavour at this particular time of year.

Choose a dry, sunny morning for picking. Don't touch the plants if they are wet, as they are likely to decay soon after you pick them, and in very strong sunshine they will tend to lose some of their volatile aromatics. Pick stalks of any plants you want to dry, sort out any dead or blemished leaves, and tie the remainder in a bundle. This can be hung up in a dry place—indoors or in a shed—for a couple of weeks until the leaves become crisp and can be crumbled between the fingers. Drying is quicker if the atmosphere is slightly warm.

Once the herbs are ready, they can be sorted out, the leaves and stalks crumbled onto a sheet of paper, and then packed into dry jars and stored. Dried herbs are about three times stronger than their fresh counterparts.

All herbs can be dried, although some are much more successful than others. Parsley is not worth the bother, and chives, French tarragon and lemon balm are not much better, but should not be totally written off. Obviously it is worth concentrating on herbs like the mints, which are dormant and cannot be picked fresh through the winter. However it is wise to have a supply of most of your herbs dried—in case of emergencies.

AUGUST

*"Tis good to be knowne
to have all of thine owne."*

From the gardener's point of view, July and August belong together. The weather and the work are likely to be the same, and there is still an abundance of crops—perhaps even more in August than July. The broad beans, early new potatoes and early peas may be coming to an end, but they will soon be replaced by runner beans, sweet corn, early tomatoes, perhaps even marrows and cucumbers. So, there is plenty to choose from, enough to feed your family with more left over to store or share with friends.

There are few tasks more enjoyable or satisfying than growing, picking and eating your own produce. It is work well done, and the results are likely to be better than anything you can buy in the shops. At least you know that the vegetables are fresh, and not contaminated with sprays. They may be odd shapes and sizes—runner beans that have curled, tomatoes that are less than perfect. This does not matter; you have only to slice open one of these tomatoes, or better still pick it from the plant and munch it like an apple, to realize that it is worth growing food for yourself.

Summary
1) Looking after crops: onions, tomatoes, celery, marrows, asparagus.
2) Sowing and planting: spring cabbage, turnips, winter radish, endive, onions.
3) Gathering, lifting and picking: runner beans, sweet corn, tomatoes, marrows, cucumbers.

Looking after crops

Many of the special jobs will follow on from last month, and you may need to adapt the timing of these to suit your own crops: when they were planted, how fast they are developing, what the weather is like and so on. But you must also be ready to deal with the following:

Onions

As your onions start to ripen, bend the leaves over to the ground to stop further growth. Stop watering them a week or so before lifting and also loosen or break the roots by levering the bulbs gently with a fork; this again stops growth and will encourage the bulbs to ripen more quickly. Any that have very thick necks should be used straight away.

Be sure to lift the crop before the bulbs start to split.

Tomatoes

Once your tomato plants have produced 4 or 5 trusses they should be stopped by nipping off the extreme tip of the stem. This prevents further upward growth and encourages the plant to divert its energy into producing fruit. If any side shoots appear where you made the cut, they must be nipped out too. From now on the fruits will develop and ripen, so the plants must be watered regularly and given liquid manure.

Celery

By August you should start to earth up trench celery. After the plants have made a few inches' growth, and when the soil is dry you can start work. First, however, you must protect the celery. Tie the sticks of each plant together just below the leaves to stop any soil getting into the hearts. Then give the trench a good watering and begin to fill it with soil from the sides, working it completely round the plants with your hands to cover about 4in of stem. After

this, continue to earth up every fortnight until the plants are completely covered except for the leaves.

If the soil is very heavy or wet it is a good idea to wrap the plants with stout paper, tied loosely around the stems, before starting to earth up.

Marrows

Make sure that you water your marrow bed regularly, and watch for the first flowers. You can easily distinguish the male and female: the latter have a very small swelling—the immature marrow—at the base of the flower, and are on very short stems. Normally fertilization is done by insects, but if you notice that the plants are not attracting any insects, and the young marrows are starting to drop off the stems, you will have to fertilize the plants by hand. Pick a male flower, strip off the petals and press the central part into the centre of

Female marrow flowers are on short stems and have a small swelling—the immature marrow—at the base of each flower.

the fully open female flower. Once some pollen has been transferred, the marrows will develop.

Asparagus

As the asparagus grows during the

summer, you may need to support the fronds. If they are broken down by the wind, growth of the roots—and therefore next year's crop—will be affected. Simply put stakes at each corner of the bed and fix two lengths of string round these, so that all the plants are surrounded and supported.

The asparagus will also need feeding. Liquid manure is good, and also seaweed. Asparagus is a shore-line plant in the wild, so seaweed is the ideal fertilizer. If you live near the sea, collect quantities from the beach and spread it on the asparagus bed. Try to pick seaweed that is not contaminated with oil stains.

Sowing and planting

Spring cabbage
In the first half of the month make the main sowings of spring cabbage. The advantage of sowing them quite late in the year is that there is less chance of the plants running to seed before they have fully developed. Sow them in the seed-bed in drills $\frac{1}{2}$in deep. If you wish, you can make two sowings at fortnightly intervals.

Turnips
Towards the end of the month, sow turnips for the early spring when the tops can be picked. Sow them in $\frac{1}{2}$in drills, intercropped between beans or peas, and sow quite thickly if you intend to grow them specifically for the tops rather than the roots.

Winter radish
These are useful for winter salads and they are hardy, large and very tasty. Grow either the Black Spanish variety which produces a root like a black-skinned turnip, or one of the Chinese varieties which produce long oval roots.

Sow them lightly in drills like summer radishes, spacing the drills 6in apart. If you sow a short row every few weeks you will get a supply of radishes from November through to March. Winter radishes need the same soil and treatment as the early varieties.

Endive
For winter salads, sow some Batavian broad-leaved endive in drills $\frac{1}{2}$in deep; the drills should be 15in apart. As the seedlings develop they should be thinned so that the plants are 15in apart. These plants for winter supplies will need to be moved to a cold frame or protected from coming frosts in October.

Onions
In some areas it is worth making an autumn sowing of onion seed at the end of August. Unless your climate is generally warm, this may be impractical, but with the right conditions, this sowing will provide you with a crop several weeks before the main spring sowing is ready, and it also tends to avoid the onion fly. However, it is important you select one of the special varieties for autumn sowing. Sow the seeds in drills $\frac{3}{4}$in deep just like the spring sowing (see p. 41) in a continuous row, but leave them unthinned until March when the first can be pulled and used as spring onions.

These onions tend to grow well until Christmas, but after that they are very vulnerable. If possible, you should construct some sort of protection for them—either a frame, cloches or any improvised structure that will prevent wind and frost from attacking the crop.

As well as the above crops, you may want to sow more perpetual spinach during August. And, if there are still green crops in the seed-bed to be planted out, they must be moved this month.

Gathering, lifting and picking

There is a real abundance of crops to choose from this month. Many from last month will still be producing during August: French beans, peas, early potatoes, perhaps some globe artichokes, cauliflowers, lettuce, beetroot, carrots, the first onions and turnips. Also a number of new crops will be ready.

Runner beans
The first pods should be ready for picking in August, and there should also be plenty of flowers on the plants. Pick the pods before they get too large and become dark green and stringy. Gather them regularly as this encourages more pods to form, and gauge the right time to pick, so that you get the best yield.

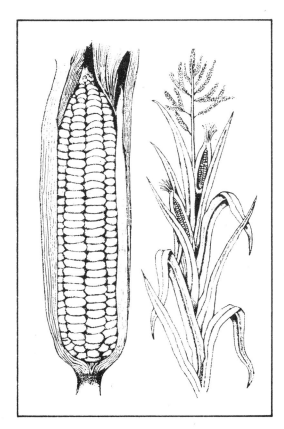

Pick sweet corn when the cobs are full and firm, and the tassel end is dark brown. The colour of the corn will vary from cream to golden yellow depending on the variety.

A good runner bean crop is a real treat during the summer. Pounds of beans can be picked nearly every day giving huge feeds for the whole family.

Sweet corn
In a hot summer, you should be able to harvest sweet corn during August. The right time to pick the cobs is when the silky tassel end has turned dark brown and the cob feels firm when held between the fingers. Break the cob from the stem of the plant, strip off the outer leaves and the tassel. The cobs should be used as soon as possible after picking. Simply wash them and cook them until the 'grains' are soft. Drench the cob in melted butter, sprinkle with salt and gnaw it between your teeth.

Once you have picked all the cobs from one plant, it can be pulled up and put on the compost heap—unless you are in a position to use it as cattle fodder.

Tomatoes
The tomatoes on the lowest trusses of the plants should be ripe during August. Pick each tomato as it becomes ripe; don't wait until a whole truss is ready. Early in the picking season there should be no problems about ripening. This will come later, when you may be left with many green tomatoes which can either be ripened indoors or used for making chutney.

There is no need to mention the many uses of tomatoes, except to say that a fresh tomato straight from the plant tastes so different from any bought variety, that it is hard to believe both belong to the same species. The plant breeders have managed to produce tomatoes that are large, very red and perfectly shaped. But the flavour has gone. I would choose a smaller, even misshapen home-grown tomato every time.

To prevent the fruit from splitting you must be sure that the soil in which the plants are growing never dries out. Splitting of the skins happens after drought when the plants are suddenly given a lot of water.

Marrows
Towards the end of the month you should be able to cut some young marrows and courgettes. If you are growing both, then it is worth using the courgettes first (when they are about 4in long), and leaving the marrows to develop, but don't let them get too large or the skins will be very hard, and the insides stringy with a lot of pith.

Cut them with a knife at the base of the stem.

Cucumbers
Protect the fruit of trailing plants by putting some straw under them. Pick the cucumbers before they get too big, while the remains of the flower are still attached to the fruit, and before any signs of yellowing occur at the stem end. Ridge cucumbers—especially small fat ones—are useful for pickling with dill and sprigs of fresh fennel.

SEPTEMBER

"Who nothing save
shall nothing have."

Early autumn. It is a turning point in the garden. By the end of the month it will be time to start thinking about and preparing for winter. There are still summer crops and summer weather, but unless you look ahead, to the end of the year, you may be short of supplies. Above all, this means giving priority to harvesting—that is gathering or lifting a whole crop in one session—storing and preserving. These will be your safeguards against winter shortage.

It is important to have enough storage space for all your crops and produce: space in the shed for hanging up strings of onions, or for suspending marrows in nets, for boxes and trays holding carrots, turnips and all the other root crops that provide food through the winter. Then in the kitchen you will need room for jars of pickles and other preserves, space for crocks of salted beans, drawers full of peas and beans—next year's seeds. And outside in a corner of the garden you may need to build clamps —storehouses for potatoes and root crops that can't be kept in the shed.

September is also the time to begin clearing up the garden, building up the compost heap, and pulling up all the crops that have finished. This month is a mixture of summer pickings and winter preparations.

Summary
1) *Looking after crops: cauliflowers, tomatoes, endive, celery.*
2) *Sowing and planting.*
3) *Gathering, picking and lifting.*

4) Harvesting, storing and preserving: onions, tomatoes, marrows, potatoes, carrots, celeriac, runner beans and French beans, saving legume seeds.
5) Preparations for winter: the compost heap, cleaning the land.

Looking after crops

There are a number of small but necessary jobs to do this month.

Cauliflowers
These will need protection, so bend the outer leaves over the curds to keep them white and to prevent dirt getting into them.

Tomatoes
If you notice that the lower leaves of your plants are withered and brown, take them off, but don't remove any healthy green leaves from *outdoor* plants as this reduces the plant's food supply, and the tomatoes will be affected.

Endive
You will need to begin blanching endive sown in June. The process takes about 3 weeks, and if it is started early in the month, the plants will be ready at a time when summer lettuces may be rather scarce. Blanching is very simple. The idea is to exclude all light from the leaves. There are several ways of blanching, and you should choose the method that suits your own needs. Do the work on a dry day, blanching a few plants at a time, and keep a look out for slugs and snails before you cover the plants. You can either put a clean, dry flower pot over each plant, covering the drainage hole with a stone to block out the light, or with large plants, bind the outer leaves over the heart and then heap straw over them. Alternatively, you can build a makeshift frame with wooden boards or tiles, and cover several plants at once. The actual design doesn't matter so long as all light is excluded and the plants themselves are not squashed or cramped.

After about 3 weeks the endives will be ready for cutting; they will have lost their bitter taste and will be ideal for salads.

Celery
Carry on earthing up the celery, bit by bit, and keep the plants well watered.

In addition to these specific jobs you should not forget to weed and hoe regularly, particularly in dry weather. Never let the soil dry out.

Sowing and planting

There is not a great deal to do this month as regards sowing and planting: a few successional sowings, and one or two winter and spring crops.

Sow some more rows of perpetual spinach, turnips for spring pickings of tops, winter radishes and lettuce. Cabbages sown early last month may need transplanting to provide crops in the spring. They can be planted in rows where potatoes have been lifted, provided the soil is firm. Plant them 18in apart, or 12in apart if a large number are planted; this is a good idea since not all the plants will survive the winter.

Gathering, lifting and picking

This month there is a build-up and continuation of crops started during July and August, with more of some and less of others. The main pickings will be runner beans, sweet corn, tomatoes, cabbages, cauliflowers, lettuce, marrows, cucumbers, carrots, turnips and beetroot.

Also you will be able to start lifting your maincrop potatoes towards the end of the month. Try to avoid leaving them in the ground for too long after the foliage has died down, as the tubers may be attacked by grubs and wireworms. They can be lifted just like earlies (see pp. 63-64). If you notice that the tops are diseased, it is best to burn them straight away; don't put them on the compost heap.

You should also try to use up any onions that have thick stems before the whole crop is lifted.

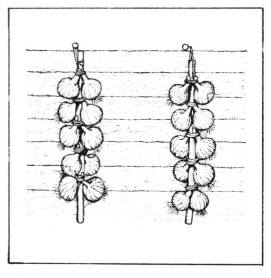

You can store onions by tying them in bundles, plaiting them or fixing them to a pole in pairs.

Harvesting, storing and preserving

Quite a number of crops mentioned above will need special treatment this month. As well as being eaten fresh, they will need to be stored and preserved for the winter.

Onions
A week or so after bending down the leaves on the onions, the whole crop can be harvested. If there are signs of wet weather, this is an urgent job. Ease the onions out of the ground with a fork. If they are ready, they will come up quite easily and the roots will be withered. Then, if the weather is fine, spread them out to dry. Lay them on some dry ground or a path, on their sides so that the base and roots are fully exposed to the sun. Cover them with sacking or a plastic sheet at night. This drying will take several days depending on the weather, and the onions must not be stored until the outer skins are brown and crisp, and the leaves have withered completely.

By far the easiest way to store onions is to hang them up in a shed, which must be dry, cool, and airy. Onions won't store well if it is warm or if they are crowded together in a sack or net. Tie them in bundles of about 6 with twine around the necks, and hang them from nails or hooks knocked into the rafters or walls of the shed. Of course, there are variations on this method: some people

tie the onions in pairs to wooden stakes which can be suspended from the ceiling, others make elaborate plaits. Any method will do so long as the onions are exposed to a free flow of air, and can be reached when needed.

Tomatoes
As the season progresses, you may find that your tomatoes are ripening very slowly. When you reach this stage, there are two things you can do: either move the plants indoors and ripen the fruit artificially, or use the green fruit for making pickles and chutneys. If you have a lot of green tomatoes you can even do both.

To ripen the tomatoes it is best to lift the whole plant and hang it upside down in a warm place with plenty of light. Or you can take off the trusses, or individual fruit, and put them on a warm window ledge indoors. Check and turn them occasionally.

You may find some tomatoes with cracked or split skins: use these straight away otherwise they will soon go mouldy. Undamaged green tomatoes —either those which you have saved, or

September

the last of the crop which stubbornly refuse to ripen—can all be turned into green tomato chutney or included in mixed pickles and piccalilli with other vegetables and fruit.

Ripe tomatoes will keep for a short while if stored on a shelf where there is a free flow of air between the fruit, no dampness and a steady, cool temperature. They need to be checked regularly for signs of decay.

Marrows

You must clear your marrow bed before the first frost strikes. Marrows will store well, so long as they are not over-ripe. Any young or immature ones should be used up quickly when the crop is finally harvested.

Store the marrows in a cool, airy place such as a shed, by suspending them from the ceiling in nets. They should keep throughout the winter provided that they are not exposed to any heat. As well as the familiar uses of marrow as a vegetable, it can be turned into chutney, jam, pickled to make 'imitation mangoes', or transformed into marrow rum by fermenting it with raisins and brown sugar.

Potatoes

Lift your maincrop potatoes when they are ready. If they are going to be stored, they should be spread out on the ground and allowed to dry off. But don't leave them for more than a couple of hours or they will begin to turn green.

For storing potatoes indoors there are certain essential requirements: darkness is important as it prevents the potatoes turning green; heat must be avoided as this will shrivel the skins and may encourage sprouting; they need ventilation or they may decay; they must be protected against thieving and scavenging animals and against frost. It is a good idea to store a sackful in the larder—provided the conditions are right—and to replenish this from your main store, which can be kept in a cool cellar or safe shed. You can pack the potatoes in boxes or sacks, covered with sacking or paper, in fact anything that will keep out light and protect the crop from frost.

If you have to store your potatoes outdoors, then the best method is to construct a clamp. I have mentioned this method in detail earlier (see pp. 24-25).

Build a potato clamp with a base of ashes and straw. Cover the potatoes with more straw and then a layer of earth.

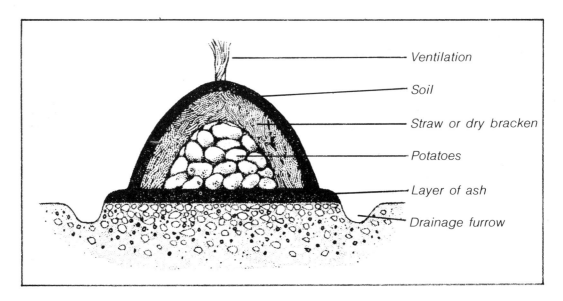

- Ventilation
- Soil
- Straw or dry bracken
- Potatoes
- Layer of ash
- Drainage furrow

September

Carrots

There is no real urgency about storing carrots this month, but if the roots are ready and the foliage is beginning to turn yellow there is no harm in lifting them. Be careful when you dig them; use a fork to loosen the roots then draw them out of the soil with your free hand. Twist off the leaves and put them on the compost heap. Don't wash or clean the roots except to remove excess earth. If you don't have a large crop, the carrots can be packed in boxes of sand. Put a layer of sand at the bottom of the box, then a layer of carrots, then another layer of sand and so on, finishing with a layer of sand. The boxes should be kept in the shed in a dry, cool atmosphere.

Large quantities of carrots can be stored in clamps outdoors (see pp. 24-25).

Celeriac

You can either leave celeriac in the ground during the winter, and dig when required, or you can lift the whole crop once the turnip-shaped roots have stopped growing. It is best to get them out if the ground tends to be wet and heavy during the winter.

Cut off the tops and store the celeriac roots either in finely sifted soil or in wood ash in boxes away from the frost and damp.

Runner beans and French beans

Both runner beans and late sowings of French beans can be salted. You will need a large crock, and about 1lb of rock or bay salt to 3lbs of beans. Put a layer of salt in the bottom of the crock and then a layer of sliced beans, then another layer of salt and so on. It is important to press down the beans as you proceed; this removes any air pockets. Finish off with a layer of salt; put a weight on the top and leave for a few days. Then, as the salt turns to brine, top up with more beans and a final layer of salt. Seal the crock and store in a dry place.

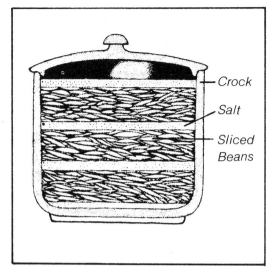

French beans and runner beans can be sliced and preserved in layers of salt.

In practice salted beans seldom keep throughout the winter, but for a couple of months at least they should provide an extra food in the kitchen, and this is a good way of making use of a surplus.

Saving legume seeds

This is a useful idea as it provides valuable seeds for next year's crops. It is possible to save the seeds from a number of vegetables like leeks and carrots, but in practice this is rarely successful. However, legumes are sturdy enough to withstand conditions that are less favourable than those provided by commercial seed merchants.

You may already have saved broad bean seeds (see p. 69) and the procedure for peas and French beans is very similar. If the weather is good, the pods can be left to ripen on the plants; if not the plants are cut off at the base of the stem and hung up indoors in a dry, airy place until the pods have turned yellow. Then they are shelled and the peas or beans put in trays to dry off; they can be left on a window sill indoors and shaken frequently. When they are hard and dry, they can be put into dry jars,

September

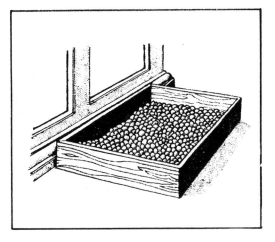

Legume seeds can be saved for sowing next year by drying them in trays on a window-sill. They should not be put in a jar or packet until completely dry.

sealed well and stored, or put into brown paper bags. In both cases the seeds should be kept away from the light.

The same procedure can be used for runner beans once they have finished and are too large for eating fresh. With the rising price of seeds any saving that you can make is worthwhile.

The compost heap
The compost heap should be almost complete by now. Next month you will need to start digging it into the soil if it is well rotted. All the remains of crops can be put onto the heap as they finish, but don't put any diseased potato foliage or hard brassica stalks on to it—these should be burned.

It is also time to get hold of a supply of farmyard manure since you will need that quite soon as well. Manure is usually quite easy to buy these days from farmers or horse owners, although you may have to collect the stuff yourself.

Clearing the land
It is too early to start any real digging yet—there are too many crops still in the soil— but you can begin to tidy up the garden ready for the onslaught next month. Clear as much rubbish as you can from the garden; rake up leaves; make bonfires.

OCTOBER

"Dull working tooles
soon courage cooles."

It is time to start using the spade again. As more and more crops are used up, the land has to be cleared and dug over. The sooner you can begin this the better. Even if you can deal with only a small patch at a time, this will give the soil a chance to be weathered and replenished through the winter, so that it will be in good condition when you start to sow again in the spring. Go steadily at this time of year, not only because October can be a warm month, but also because this is the first really heavy work for several months. Digging and clearing an established plot, though, is easy compared with the first onslaught on a piece of wild uncultivated grassland which may need scything, slashing brambles, barrowing rubble, raking—different jobs for a whole battery of tools and equipment.

As you harvest and store more crops you will need to organize your eating habits so that the hardiest crops like leeks are used as late as possible. Try to start your winter food with the cabbages and cauliflowers that have to be cleared from the land, and then gradually work through your stored crops: roots like carrots, beetroot, celeriac, and so on, together with crops that can be stored in the soil. Planning and good sense are the answers to this problem.

Summary
1) Work on the land: clearing and digging, asparagus, celery, leeks, brassicas, endive, peas and runner beans.

2) Last summer crops and pickings: runner beans, savoys, spinach.
3) Lifting and storing: beetroot, turnips, kohl-rabi, salsify.

Work on the land

Clearing and digging
As areas of your plot are cleared of crops, start to dig through them and add manure when necessary. It is particularly important to start digging heavy soil as early as possible. Sandy, light soils can be left until after Christmas.

If you want to extend your plot, make a start by double-digging any uncultivated grassland before the weather becomes too bad (see p. 14).

Asparagus
By now the asparagus will have stopped growing, the foliage will start to turn brown and can be cleared. Cut down all the stems to within a few inches of the ground, leaving a small portion to show where the crowns are situated. Burn all the foliage. During the summer plenty of weeds will have sprung up, so clear these and give the bed a dressing of manure or seaweed covered with a thin layer of soil. The bed can then be left for the winter.

Celery
During October you should finish earthing up the trench celery, and once the soil has covered all the stems, leaving only the foliage showing, the earth can be firmed and smoothed to produce a solid ridge; this will help to divert any rain. If there is a danger of frost, it is best to protect the tops with a layer of straw.

Leeks
Leeks planted out earlier in the year will be growing well. Earth them up even if they were planted in holes. This gives support and protection to the plants and helps to produce long blanched stems.

Cabbages, brussels sprouts and cauliflowers
All these winter greens will need some attention. Hoe them well and firm the soil, particularly around the sprout plants. Also draw a little earth around the base of the stalks to support the plants. Protect the heads of cauliflowers with outer leaves from the plants.

The sprouts will be forming well, but don't be tempted to pick them too early; wait until they are very firm. As the leaves at the base of the plants begin to turn yellow, remove them and put them on the compost heap.

Endive
Carry on with blanching the early sowings of endive, keeping a watch for slugs and snails that lurk around the plants. The late sowings of Batavian endive, which have to stand out during the winter, will need to be moved to a frame or covered with cloches to protect the plants from frost.

Peas and runner beans
Once these are finished, pull up the pea sticks and bean poles, and store them in a dry place for the winter. Throw out any that are broken or rotten. These stakes are very useful and you should look after them; it is very frustrating to go hunting for sticks at the last moment, when your crops are already toppling over.

Last summer crops and pickings

Runner beans
You may still be able to pick a few runner beans at the beginning of the month, although they are likely to be fairly stringy. After this, pick the pods and dry them for seeds. Then pull up the plants, disentangling the twining stems

from the poles. Burn the roots and put the stems and foliage on the compost heap.

Savoy cabbages

The first of these may be ready for cutting, depending on the climate and the time you planted them. But they will provide a useful supply of fresh greens through the winter and possibly right up to March.

Spinach

The first sowings of perpetual spinach may be ready for picking. Even if you only take a few outer leaves, this will help the plants to produce more.

You should also be able to pick blanched endive, young parsnips, cauliflowers and cabbages.

Lifting and storing

Any crops that are still in the soil and are not likely to withstand the winter should be lifted and stored as soon as possible. These include potatoes, carrots, beetroot, turnips, kohl-rabi, celeriac, and salsify. Swedes can be left until December before lifting, and other crops can be left in the soil until required: celery, leeks, Jerusalem artichokes and parsnips.

I mentioned potatoes, carrots and celeriac last month. The others will need attention for the first time this month.

Beetroot

Large beetroot should not be left in the ground too long otherwise they may become tough and fibrous. Lift them by plunging a spade under the roots to loosen them, and then pull them out carefully with your free hand. Be careful not to bruise or gash the roots; any that are damaged should be used up quickly. Twist off the leaves just above the root. The easiest way of storing them

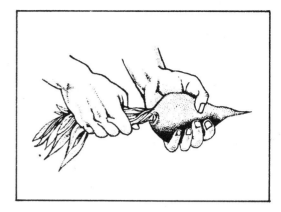

Be careful not to damage beetroot when you dig them, and twist off the leaves or they will 'bleed'.

is to put them in boxes in layers with sifted soil or dry ashes. The boxes should be stored in a shed or cellar, protected from damp and frost.

If you have a very large crop of beetroot, you can store them like carrots in clamps (see pages 24-25).

Turnips

Turnips sown earlier in the year, specifically for winter storing, can be lifted and dealt with like beetroot. If the

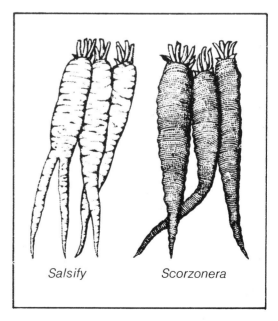

Salsify   *Scorzonera*

Salsify and scorzonera can make useful additions to your winter root crops.

roots from later sowings don't develop, leave the plants in the soil, and pick the tops in the spring.

Kohl-rabi

These can be left in the ground over the winter, as they are very hardy, but they tend to lose their flavour and texture if they are allowed to grow too big. They are best when they are the size of turnips. Lift the plants and take off the outer leaves—these can be cooked like cabbage—and store the swollen bulbs in boxes of wood ash in a damp-proof shed or cellar.

Salsify (and scorzonera)

These can be left in the ground, but it is safer and more convenient to lift and store them. Dig out the roots with a fork, being careful not to damage them, as they are very long. Twist off the tops and store the roots like carrots in boxes of sand.

NOVEMBER

"For herbs good store,
trench garden more."

There is no doubt now that winter has arrived. All the summer crops are finished, and the pleasant autumn weather has changed, giving way to the cold, dark days of November. You will need to spend most of this month digging and manuring the ground. Start to think about next year's crops and work out roughly how you can rotate them. Aim to have one third of the land dug over and manured before Christmas. Then there is the onion bed to deal with; this is usually a separate job, needing early deep digging and treading.

But the month isn't all sweat and heavy digging. More winter vegetables will be ready for use. As well as stored crops, you can begin to pull leeks and celery, and also pick the first brussels sprouts—a real sign that winter has begun.

From now on work in the garden will be determined by the weather. If it is bad, then you may be housebound, unable to get outside for several days, so don't waste time when you have the opportunity of getting some useful work done.

Summary
1) *Digging and clearing: general digging, the onion bed, lime, herbs.*
2) *Sowing: broad beans.*
3) *Protection of crops: cauliflowers, celery and parsnips.*
4) *New crops and pickings: brussels sprouts, red cabbage, celery, leeks,*

87

parsnips, Jerusalem artichokes.
5) *Stores: clamps, other stores.*

Digging and clearing

General digging
It makes sense to get well ahead with digging while the weather is still favourable. This month you should aim to have one third of the patch dug and manured. This will be one part of the rotation for next year's crops (see p. 15). Where possible you should double dig unless the land has been under cultivation for quite some time. Add plenty of manure and compost as you work through the patch. Generally it is best to throw the soil up in ridges or to dig rough; this doesn't imply that the ground should be full of humps and hollows, but simply that the soil is turned over and left without breaking up the clods. The overall surface should be fairly level.

The onion bed
This is the other major digging job that must be done before Christmas. If you have an established onion bed and the crops are not troubled by pests or disease, you can keep this bed outside the normal rotation and use it year after year, providing that it is well dug each winter. If you have had trouble with pests, or want to include onions in your rotation for convenience, they can be grown in soil used previously for a crop like carrots or runner beans, where the land has been well dug. In these cases the soil should be turned over roughly, but no major work is necessary.

However, if you are making a new onion bed, deep digging and manuring are essential. Choose a sunny position and dig to about 18in, incorporating as much manure, compost and decayed greenstuff as possible. This should be put in at the bottom of the trench and should be several inches below the surface. Leave the soil in ridges until the spring when it can be levelled, raked and firmed before planting.

Lime
Normally a dressing of lime can be given every three years, but you will need to put on more if your soil is sour (see p. 13), if there is a tendency to produce club root in cabbages or if the climate is very rainy. About 6-8 oz of powdered limestone per sq yd can be forked lightly into the soil, either now or after Christmas, so long as it does not coincide with manuring. Don't lime soil where potatoes are to be grown as this may produce scab on the tubers.

Herbs
Clean up the herb garden. Cut down mint, remove all dead twigs and branches from other herbs that are dormant through the winter, and trim the big bushy herbs like sage and thyme.

Sowing

Broad beans
It is worth making one sowing of broad beans in November, but make sure that you choose one of the autumn varieties. Sow them in staggered rows as before (see p. 35). The advantage of an autumn sowing is that you will be able to pick beans at the end of May if you are lucky. Also the plants are not vulnerable to attack from blackfly as they flower early.

The plants are quite hardy and will usually withstand frost, but it is worth covering them with some straw if the weather is very bad.

Protection of crops

Cauliflowers
Cauliflowers and heading broccoli can be protected from winter frost by heeling

November

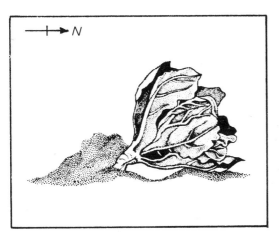

Heel over cauliflowers and broccoli to protect them from frost.

Pick brussels sprouts from the bottom of the stalk, working upwards.

them over so that they point north. Take some earth from the 'north side' of the plants and pile it on the stem—on the other side—at the same time bending the whole plant over, but not dislodging the roots. The aim of this is to prevent the sudden thawing of frozen plants when they are exposed to the full sun.

Celery and parsnips
If there is a danger of frost, it is advisable to protect the tops of celery and parsnips in the soil, by covering them with straw. Globe artichokes will also need some protection.

New crops and pickings

This month there will be pickings of perpetual spinach, endive, winter cabbages and savoys, cauliflowers, and some new crops will also be ready.

Brussels sprouts
Sprouts can be picked as soon as they are tight and firm. Work from the bottom of the plants upwards, picking a few of the best sprouts from each. The easiest method is to cut the sprouts from the stems with a sharp knife. This is clean and quick.

Red cabbage
Whether you grow a few red cabbages for pickling, eating raw in salads or cooking as a vegetable, let the frost season them before you cut any. Strip off any loose outer leaves and use only the heads. They are perfect at this time of year.

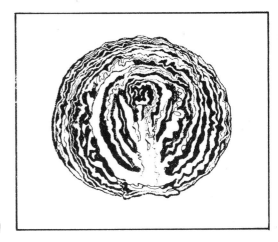

Pickle red cabbage once it has been seasoned by the frost.

Celery
You can start to use celery in November. However, be careful when you lift the plants. Work along the rows and scrape the soil from one side of each plant

before you plunge a spade down and under the roots. The whole plant can then be levered out of the soil.

Self-blanching celery can be lifted quite simply with a fork, but remember that these plants are not hardy and you must watch for any signs of frost.

Leeks
Once they are large enough you can start to lift leeks like celery, using a spade to scrape away the soil from one side of the plants. The leeks can then be pulled and levered out of the soil.

Parsnips
The longer these can be left in the ground the better. Exposure to frost increases their sugar content so they have a better flavour later in the year.

The best way of lifting parsnips is to begin at one end of the row and gradually work your way along it. Dig a hole about 1ft deep at the end of the row, scrape the soil away from the first parsnip into this hole. Once the parsnip has been loosened it can be pulled out without breaking the root. This will leave a hole in front of the next root which can be dealt with in the same way.

Jerusalem artichokes
Cut down and clear the stems this month and then begin to dig the tubers. Use a fork and lift them like potatoes as you want them.

Stores

Clamps
Check these and secure them for the winter. Bank and firm the soil around them. You do not want them to collapse or to be vulnerable to the weather. Look at them occasionally—particularly after heavy rain—when the soil may have been disturbed and will need banking up again.

Other stores
As the supply of fresh greens from the garden begins to run out, you can start to use root crops from your stores: potatoes, carrots, turnips, etc. All the boxes and sacks in store should be checked and any soft or mouldy vegetables thrown out straight away.

Look after your winter root crops and store them well. If kept in suitable conditions they will retain their quality for several months.

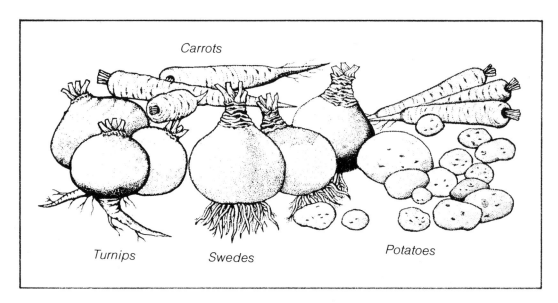

Carrots

Turnips   Swedes   Potatoes

DECEMBER

"Good husband and housewife, now chiefly be glad,
things handsome to have, as they ought to be had."

The end of the year. But the garden doesn't come to a stand-still. There is always work to be done. The main job is to carry on with the digging and general tidying up of the plot. Also you must fight the weather, anticipate frosts or gales and protect your crops. You will have been aware of the weather throughout the whole year, but now you must be even more watchful.

At Christmas you can either relax and do no work on principle, or it may be an opportunity to catch up with some of the jobs which still need to be completed. In either case you cannot afford to forget the garden *completely*. If you are not outside working, then think and plan indoors.

But this doesn't mean that you should not enjoy Christmas. Now that the year's work is done, you can sit back for a while and perhaps think about what you have produced. If you look outside, the garden may seem bleak, even barren, but indoors—in the shed and the kitchen—there will be enough food, with luck, to see you through the worst weather.

Summary
1) *General work: digging, leaves, planning.*
2) *Fighting the weather: wind and gales, frost, young crops.*
3) *Picking and storing: swedes, crops in store.*

December

General work

Digging
Carry on with digging whenever the weather permits. Make full use of good days for getting the work done, so that you don't have to rush early next year. Along with digging you should clear rubbish from the garden, keeping all that can be put to rot for the compost heap. Pull up any old stumps of greens when they are finished and burn them for wood ash.

Leaves
Collect leaves regularly from October onwards and either put them onto the compost heap, or make separate enclosures for leaf-mould. Leaf-mould takes time to mature into useful humus, but it is a valuable conditioner and mulch after a year or so.

Planning
The records that you have been keeping through the year will be almost complete, and now is a good time to start looking at them in detail, and planning next year's work. See if any crops failed, and try to establish why. Look at the successes and failures, and make alterations to your yearly plan if necessary. It is not too early to begin ordering seeds—in fact the earlier this can be done the better.

Fighting the weather

Wind and gales
These are treacherous and you must try to protect your crops against them. Natural windbreaks like hedges will help tremendously at this time of year, but failing this, you will have to build some sort of artificial windbreak, which can be set along the windward side of your crops. Wattle hurdles used to be common, but nowadays you may have to be content with a 'hedge' made of twigs and branches. Or you can put up some strong wooden boards—a kind of temporary fence—so long as they will withstand the power of the wind.

Frost
This is the other enemy in December. If you think that a hard frost is imminent, then you must lift celery and parsnips before the frost comes and hardens the ground. Lift enough for a week or two so that you don't need to dig any more for a while. Cover the tops of the remaining plants with straw if you have not already done this.

The main thing with frost, as with other bad weather, is to be ready for it. In the case of frost, this means having a supply of straw handy for covering crops, also sacking for protecting crops in store.

But there is one advantage of frosty weather. Since it makes the ground very hard, barrowing is much easier. Make use of frosty days then, for moving manure, compost and anything else.

Young crops
The two main crops that will need to be watched are broad beans and spring cabbage. The broad beans sown in the autumn will have grown a few inches; draw a little soil around the plants, but generally they are quite hardy. Spring cabbages should also be earthed up. If the weather has been mild, they may have been developing quickly; in this case you should cut them, or they will spoil when the weather changes.

Picking and storing

There should still be plenty of crops in the ground and ready for picking: brussels sprouts, savoys, spinach, celery, Jerusalem artichokes, leeks and parsnips.

December

Savoys can be cut from November until March.

Swedes

Although these are very hardy and can be left in the ground right through the winter, it may be more convenient to lift them this month, so that the ground can be dug over. It is best to use them before they get too large, or they will be tough and stringy.

Lift the swedes, and cut off the leaves. They can be stored in wood ash like other root crops, in a shed or cellar.

Crops in store

All the crops that are stored in nets, trays or boxes should be checked occasionally and all mouldy specimens thrown out straight away.

At the end of the year, your shed should be filled with stored produce—onions, marrows, potatoes, root crops, trays of shallots—as well as your tools.

Starting Again

Once Christmas is over, and the new year has begun, you must get back to work in the garden. You can afford to have some time away from the plot in December, but in January you must do as much as you can. Outside, there is plenty of digging and tidying up to do ready for the spring sowings. Indoors, you will need to make plans: how to improve your garden and crops in the coming year; assessing what went wrong last year and how to avoid making the same mistakes again. If you have kept records, the evidence should be there.

Winter weather can delay work, but remember the year is ahead, for more experiments, more sowing, planting, picking, storing and preserving. What you do in the first weeks will affect the whole year's work, so you *must* lever yourself out of your armchair, go out and start once again.

Three-year
cropping plans
may be drawn to
scale on the following
squared pages.

Your own Plot

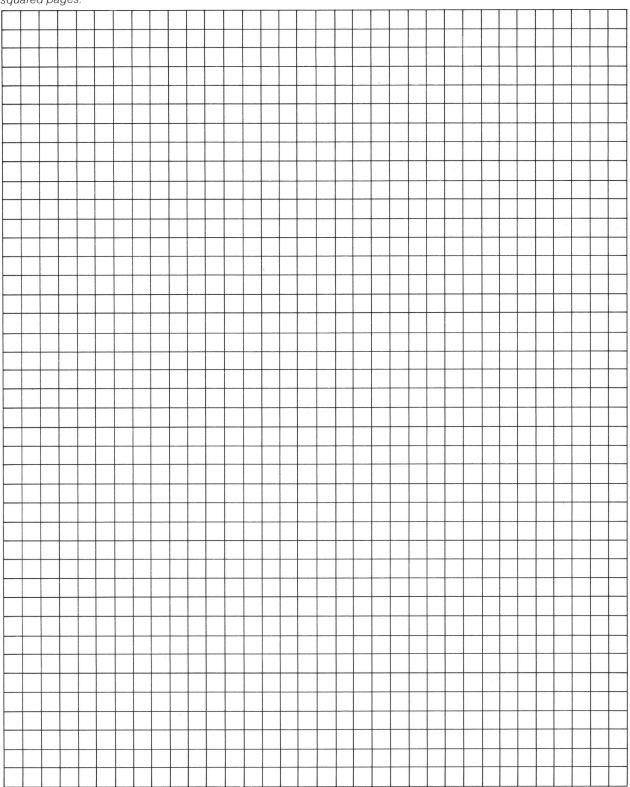

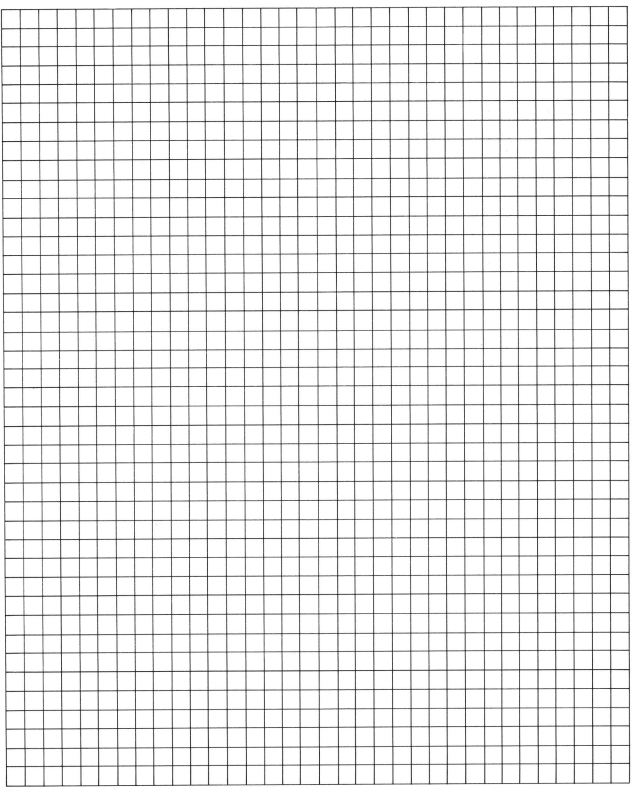

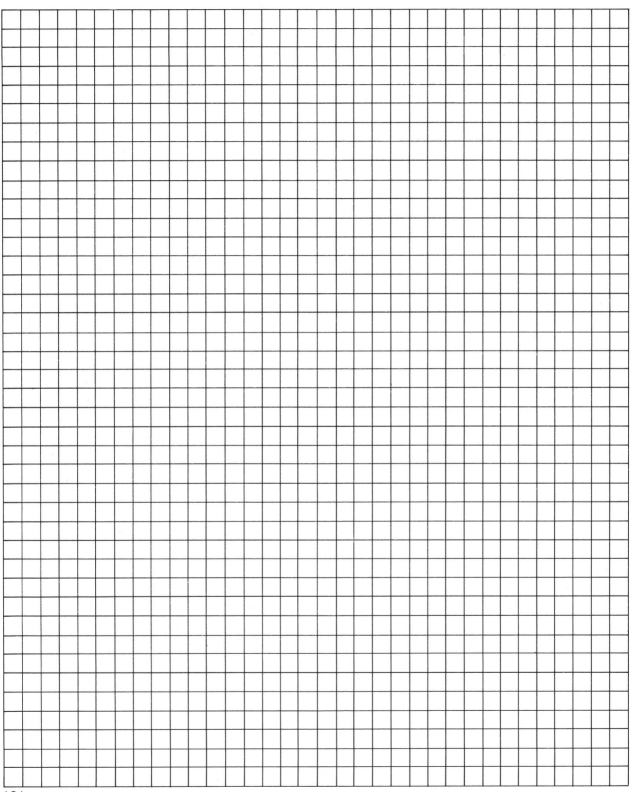

Index

Index

Index